Teac ms-i
Tabrezi

(Rumi's Master)

Prof.Dr. Erkan TÜRKMEN

NKM

Teachings of Shams-i Tabrezi

Research Series: 55

November 2009

Director of publication: **İsmail Çalışkan**
Director of art: **Ömer Tekiner**

ISBN 978-9944-116-95-4

Cover designed by: **Harun YILDIZ**

Preprinting preparation: **Mehmet ATEŞ**
meh_ates@hotmail.com

Press: **Sebat Ofset Matbaacılık**

LIBRARY CARD
- Cataloging in Publication Data (CIP) -

TÜRKMEN, Erkan
Teachings of Shams-i Tabrezi

ANAHTAR KAVRAMLAR
- key concepts -

1. Shams-i Tabrezi, 2. Mevlana, 3. Sufism, 4. Mysticism

NKM
www.nuvekultur.com
nuve@nuvekultur.com
literaturk@nuvekultur.com
romantikkitap@gmail.com
ilkkitap@gmail.com

M. Muzaffer Cad. Rampalı Çarşı Alt Kat No: 35-36-41
Meram / KONYA
Tel: 0.332.352 23 03 Fax: 0.332.342 42 96

Alemdar Mah. Himaye-i Etfal Sok. Aydoğmuş Han Nu. 7/G
Cağaloğlu / İSTANBUL
Telefaks 0.212.511 37 86

Teachings of Shams-i Tabrezi

(Rumi's Master)

Prof.Dr. Erkan TÜRKMEN

NKM

Prof.Dr. Erkan TÜRKMEN

Dr. Türkmen was born in Peshawar, India (now in Pakistan) in 1943. His parents had immigrated from Turkmenistan, Merv. He belongs to a noble family in India. His grandfather Mirza Feridun Beg was deputy superintendent of Jalandhar city India. Dr.Türkmen studied at the Muslim Anglo Oriental College, Lahore and left the college to migrate to Turkey in 1962. In 1972, he graduated from the Faculty of Arts and Sciences, Department of English Language and Literature, Ankara Unicersity in 1972.

In 1979 he got his Ph.D. Degree from Istanbul University, Department Eastern Languages and Literature (Persian Literature). He taught English, Persian and Turkish Literature at the Seljuk University, Konya. There he wrote his book on Rumi: The Essence of Rumi's Masnevi based on commentaries written in Urdu, Turkish, Persian and English. At Seljuk University he got the titles of Associate and Full Professorahip.

Dr. Türkmen worked and carried out his research in India, Kazakistan, Libya, North Cyprus and Iran. He wrote his articels in Urdu, Persian, Turkish and English. He taught the literature of the same languages at various universities. He attended many international conferences in Turkey, Iran, India, Pakistan, Singapore, North Cyprus, Turkmenistan and Kazakistan.

He worked as Vice Rector and Dean at the 18 Mart University Çanakkale and as Dean at the Çağ University, Mersin. Presently he is working at Çağ University, Faculty of Arts and Sciences..

Other Publications of the Author:

1	The Esence Of Rumi's Masnevi, 1. Baskı, Kültür ve Turizm Bakanlığı Yayınları, Ankara, 2002; 2. Baskı, Eris Yayınları, Konya, 2004.
2	Besinnung Sufi Dichter Rumis Schönster Verse, Anadolu Manşet Gazetesi Yayınları, Konya, 2004.
3	Teaching Of Shams-i Tabrezi (Rumi's Master), Anadolu Manşet Gazetesi Yayınları, First Press, Konya, 2004: Second Press, NKM, Konya, 2009.
4	Şems-i Tebrîzi'nin Öğretileri, 1. Baskı, Anadolu Manşet Gazetesi Yayınları, Konya, 2004; 2. Baskı, NKM, Konya, 2007; 3. Baskı, NKM, Konya, 2009.
5	Mevlâna Mesnevisi'nin Evrenselliği, NKM, Konya, 2007.
6	Son Darbe, NKM, Konya, 2007.
7	Sultan Raziye, NKM, Konya, 2007.
8	Mevlâna'nın Öğretileri, NKM, Konya, 2009.

PREFACE

Mevlana (our master) Jelal al-Din Rumi (1207- 1273) was a learned Muslim scholar, a teacher, jurisprudent and a respected mufti until he met with a Sufi Shams-i Tabrezi in 1244. The meeting brought an upheaval in the life of Rumi (the Anatolian). He gave up all of his titles and names and began to follow his master in whom he discovered mysteries of divine love. He wrote a huge *Divan* (collection of poems) dedicated to him.

Some Maqalat (discourses) of Shams throw light upon what he gave to Rumi, that lacked before their meeting. Shams' discourses may look old fashioned, but they can still guide to those who are seeking reality without being captivated in the narrow boundaries of religions.

Shams had a shrewd mind and wisdom of criticism; and he was able to understand people's characters by analyzing their problems. He chose no Sheikh, no nationality and no country like a true Sufi. He claimed to be the beloved of God chosen by Him, which opened a new page in the Islamic Mysticism.

Rumi could not be Rumi without Shams as he says:

Nothing can itself be anything,

No iron can be a sword on its own,

Neither could Rumi's spiritual Masnevi be born

Without his being a slave of Shams-i Tabrezi.

by

Prof.Dr. Erkan TÜRKMEN

Çağ Üniversitesi

Yenice, Mersin, Turkey

CONTENTS

BIOGRAPHY OF SHAMS-I TABREZI

Biography of Shams-i Tabrezi:

(The architect of Rumi's spiritual world).

"You are the moon of the sky and we are like a dark night, and when there is no moon at night full darkness prevails." (Divan-i Shams p. 711/ 1889).

Shams al-Din Muhammad son of Ali bn Melikdad was born at Tabriz probably in 1184. Shams caused a great storm over the spiritual ocean of Rumi, when they first met in 1244 in Konya. The most authentic sources of his own life are his discourses that we shall render here, Rumi's great Divan (a collection of his love poems) and Sultan Veled's (Rumi's son's) statements found in his "Velednama". Sipahsalar and Ahmed Eflaki Dede's works are of secondary importance.

Although Shams' discourses throw significant light on his life and on his relation with Rumi, which forms the essential part of this book, yet a short introductory history of his life seems to be necessary to understand the relation of his discourses with his life.

When Shams was a child, he had a strange state, which even his father failed to understand. He would say to his son "You are not mad! Then what kind of religion do you have? You did not have any spiritual training or discipline to follow this way" My answer to this remark used to be, "You and I are like a hen with chickens and I am an egg of a duck bred under the hen with other chicks. I can jump into the (spiritual) sea, as I am an aquatic bird. If you belonged to my kind, you could also do the same"

(Makalat,Tur. p. 42 and Franklin p.142). He learnt Arabic and Fıkh during his stay at Damascus. He studied theology and different sects of Islam (see Makalat p. 87-88; 243; 303.) He taught the subjects but finally he gave up the job to be a real Sufi. After that he began to travel from town to town in search of God loving men. For this reason he was called "Shams al-Din-i Perinde" (The flying sun of religion). He would wear a black robe of felt and would stay at Hans (hotels). When he met with Awhaduddin Kirmani in Baghdad, he asked him "What is your problem?" The sheikh replied, "I am trying to see the moon in the water of a basin". Upon this Shams said, "Well do you have a boil on your neck. Can't you see the moon directly? Now you should find a doctor, who could treat you and make you look at the realities as they are." This shows the difference between their views. Kirmani believed in beauty of forms and would worship young boys' charming faces (for details see Essence of Rumi, p. 33).

Shams was a disciple of Sheikh Ebu Bakir Sillabaf for some time, who failed to discover his spiritual world. He left the Sheikh for the following reason " Sheikh Abu Bekir's intoxication came from God, but he did not posses the sobriety that comes after that intoxication" (Makalat, Tur.p. 204) Shams had met with many Sheikhs and had developed a talent for understanding them at one glance.

Junction of The Two Oceans

On the 23rd October 1244 Rumi and Shams met with each other. The story of their meeting differs in Aflaki and Sipahsalar's statements slightly and there is also some information given in the Makalat of Shams. We can join the event: 'One day when Rumi was going towards Pembefurushan Inn he passed by Shekerizan Street on the back of a mule, where Shams stopped him and asked him "O the great Imam of Islam! Tell me who is greater, Prophet Muhammad or Bayazid of Bastam?" Rumi replied, "What kind of question is this? Of course, Muhammad is greater than Bayazid." Shams continued, "Muhammad said 'O my Lord I fail to understand You the way You really deserve, but Bayazid said 'How great is my being, and I am the king of kings. I am free from all defects and there is nothing left in my robe other than God'. What do you think about it?" Rumi said, "Well the thirst of Bayazid was quenched by one drop, and his jar of wisdom was filled with that; and the light he received was just in accordance with the capacity of his window of divine light while Muhammad's thirst was huge and at every stage he wanted more and more love and knowledge of God according to the Koranic verse 'Didn't We expand your chest?' (94/1) and 'Was not the earth of God spacious enough to escape evil? (4/97) (Eflaki II/218-219) ".

Upon this Shams shouted and Rumi almost fell from the Mule's back. After this dialogue Rumi and Shams went to the house of Selah al-Din Zerkub, where they stayed for some months talking and discussing divine matters; and exchanging thousands of questions and answers (Eflaki p.622-623). They also performed Sema (the transcendental dance). Husammeddin Chelebi, who noted down the Masnevi for Rumi, also gave up all his wealth for Shams and became his loving disciple and joined them (Eflaki p.627).

"Shams led Rumi from the stage of a lover to the stage of a beloved of God (Velednama, Tur.p 249 and Per. p 197).

"Shams said to him: Although you have already discovered the secrets of your inner self, listen! I am the inner self of inner self, secrets of secrets; and lights of lights" (ibid. Per.p 197).

"The Sheikh (Rumi) became a student in his presence. He learnt many lessons, and although he had studied many subjects before, he began with Shams like a newly registered student. He was a guide before, now he was a student. Shams took him to a strange world, which had been seen neither by an Arab nor by a Turk (ibid. p 198).

Rumi invited Shams to his house saying "This house does not deserve you, but I sincerely love you; whatever I have is yours, doubtless you are the true master (ibid.Per. p 42).

Rumi's son Veled continues to throw light upon their relationship. He says that their meeting was like Khızr and Moses. Prophet Moses was a knowledgeable man but he was told by God to meet with a person (the Prophet Khizr) whose knowledge was endless for he received it directly from God (see the Koran 18/60-82). Rumi received this kind of knowledge from Shams.

After Shams' arrival, Rumi gave up delivering his beautiful sermons, which made his disciples angry and they bore enmity towards Shams. Rumi beside his regular prayers began to perform Sema in the company of musicians and Qawal (hymn singers), which looked non- Islamic to the fanatic. The fundamentalists thought that their Sheikh, son of a great Muslim imam, had gone astray from Sheriah (Islamic Law) (See Eflaki 3/83 and Velednama, Per. p. 43). When the opposition reached its prime, especially with the scandals of the Akhi sect, Shams left Konya and went to Damascus. Sultan Veled gives the following details:

People said, "He (Rumi) opened our eyes and made us see and turned our hearts knowledgeable like that of Avicenna, who then is this man (Shams), who has taken our sheikh from us like the stream-water that carries away a husk? Maybe he is a wizard who has cast his spell on our sheikh and has tied him to himself. Shams neither belongs to a renowned family nor do we know from where he has come" (Velednama, Per. p. 43).

Unable to bear the pain of separation, Rumi went mad. He was destitute and was like Zanun (of Egypt, a great Sufi d. in A.D. 859) because of love. Now, sheikh and mufti had become a poet, and an intoxicated lover not by the wine made of grapes but by the spiritual wine of divine light, which he often drank. He kept dancing, performing Sema day and night; and turned around on earth like a wheel. His yearnings and cries rose up to the sky to be heard by all the young and the old. He gave away golden and silver coins and whatever he possessed to the musicians and singers, until they were tired and their throats were swollen. There rose a great tumult in the world and people said, "Such a great scholar of Islam and the imam of this world and the other has begun to recite poems and people have given up Sheriah and followed him for love. All those who once recited the Koran have now begun to sing and dance. Love has become their religion and faith. They don't care for believers or non-believers. All they look for is love and Shams has become their only Lord" (Velednama p. 52).

After some time, Rumi sent his son Veled to Damascus with a letter to fetch Shams. When Veled found him in Damascus, he also, like his father, was lured by the charming talk of the master. As he says: "Shams began to speak and cast pearls out of his mouth. He sowed new love in my heart and soul. He, by speaking about the Koran and Traditions of Muhammad, disclosed some secrets. He made me fly in the sky without wings, and took me close to God's throne (*Arsh*). He undid the curtains of my eyes to turn my night into a day.

He took me to the sea that had no boundaries; and where I found peace of heart. There I felt like a bird freed from its cage and safe from all kinds of dangers *(Velednama, p.48)*.

When Sultan Veled read the letters (for versified letters see Eflaki 11.p.701) and gave presents to Shams, he agreed to come back to Konya. They set out on the journey. On the way, Veled did not ride on horseback for the sake of respect to his father's master. When they arrived in Konya on the 8th of May 1247 (see ibid p. 48) a great mob was waiting to receive them. Rumi's disciples apologized for what they had done before. Rumi began to recite poems about Shams, which were later collected as "Divan-i Shams-i Tabrezi".

Here are some of his verses about Shams:

"Shams is an appetizer and wine, he is a *Chang* and a *Rubab;* he is drink and intoxication, and light and fire. He is not the kind of fire that brings forth sorrow, sadness or repentance, but he is a kind of intoxication that increases self-respect and pride" (Divan p. 427).

"Shams has appeared and held a meeting in my heart and due to the wine of (divine) love, these walls and doors have gone mad" (Divan p. 189).

"The proof of the sun is the sun itself, if you are looking for proof then don't turn your face away from the sun" (M.1/116).

"Be silent, so that you may hear from that sun which you can't find in books or in discourses" (M.III/ 1306).

Shams was not understood by the society around him in Konya as he says in his discourses:

"These people are right not to understand my words because my words come from the side of God... Let me tell you something: These people like hypocrisy, and righteousness makes them uneasy. Once I said to a person 'You are the most unique and the greatest fellow on the earth'. He held my hand and said, "I was yearning to see you, but I was remiss in not finding you". A year later when I told him the reality, he became angry and my enemy. However, it is not so unusual! In order to live happily among these people you have to be a hypocrite but if you always want to tell the truth, you have to live in a desert or on a mountain" (Makalat, Tur.p.61)

"These imams (the Muslim priests) do not understand even the exoteric meanings of the Koran, while to understand the esoteric meanings of the Koran one needs the light of belief and not the fire of show. If they had (the true) belief, they would not seek the rank of Imam for wealth or money" (Makalat, Per. p. 66).

Nevertheless, scandals spread again, and the orthodox Muslims and the anti government Turcomans thought that Shams was damaging Islamic belief, therefore, they decided to get rid of him once for all. Now there are two stories about Shams' disappearance: either he left the town in December, 1247 for ever or he was assassinated by a gang of seven persons, who called Shams out while Rumi and his master were talking in privacy (as told by Eflaki), but Veled says that Shams disappeared forever. The later assumption seems to be more accurate because Rumi went to Damascus twice in search of his master and failed to find him (Veled p. 61). Moreover, Rumi after waiting for some years went to Damascus as Veled says, which leads us to believe that Shams really disappeared because Rumi could not be so naïve as to remain unaware of the fate of his master.

Finally, Rumi gave up looking for Shams and found him within himself:

"He (Rumi) said: Since I am him then why I am looking for him. I am just like him and I shall speak on my own. When you know your sheikh well, you know God without curtains" (Veled p. 61-62).

TEACHINGS OF SHAMS

Unlike Rumi Shams wrote no books. His discourses or sermons (*Maqalat)* are a collection of his speeches that he delivered during his stay at Konya, and were composed by his disciples including Rumi. The discourses are like puzzles and, most of the time, lead nowhere. Therefore, his teachings given in this book comprise only those that are didactic or throw light on Shams' life and his relation with Rumi. There are two sources for the purpose: The Turkish translation (shown here as *Tur.*) of M. Nuri Gençosman (Hürriyet Yayınevi, Istanbul). The translation though not accurate is based on different and reliable manuscripts that the translator compared, especially those that are available at the Mevlana Museum Library (No. 2144 and 2145). The other source is of 'Ahmed Khushnawis' *Maqalat-i Shams-i Tabrezi* Tehran, Iran (here shown as *Per.*).

On God:

1- Love buys eternity:

When we pass away from this body, we reach the soul, which is created (*Hathis*) while God is not a Created Being and is Eternal (*Qadim*). How can a created one find the Creator and the Eternal?

Man is made of clay (minerals) and God is the Omni Creator. Then how can man be His equal? The power that puts you to struggle and leads you to freedom is the soul, and if you endanger your life for this aim it will be of no use:

If lovers bring to you their souls as presents,
Their sacrifice will be like taking cumin to Kirman.

If you take cumin to Kirman (where cumin grows in abundance), what value or price does it have? Such is the gate of God! God has no needs and desires. So, take your desires (supplications) to Him. He, who has no desires, will like to have them. Because of this supplication you can free yourself of the events you don't want around you. Then you will earn something of divine eternity, which is love. Now you will be entrapped by love that will tie you up as God says in the Koran: "God loves them and they love Him (5/54)". Through this eternity you may find a further way to it as is said, "His grasp is over all visions (6/103)" This is the gist of all ideas, which of course has no end and will continue to manifest until the last day (Per. 17/ Tur. 32).

Notes: The full Koranic verse 5/54 is 'O you who believe! If any from you turn his back from his faith, soon God will produce people whom he will love and they will love Him'. The verse No.6/103 is: 'No vision can grasp Him, but His grasp is over all visions. He is above all comprehension, yet He is acquainted with all things'.

2- Empty your hearts for God:

'When your wholeness is absorbed in God's wholeness, and when your whole being is occupied by Him', it is then the time to look for Him actively. He is the kind of God, who has created the sky (universe) in which the whole wisdom is lost; and one cannot understand even a star properly. There are many philosophers, astrologists and scientists who have said many things about the stars but what they say is not always true. A star has come out of the same universe from which the others have come out. Then what sort of universe is this? Even a beetle living in dung wants to see and know God. Many lovers have sacrificed their lives in search of God and their lives shattered. They came down from the other world (like the stars) while the other world keeps an eye on them until they desire to die so that God may give them a new life. For God, they give up all of their possessions and fame like the prince Abu bin Edhem (Per.p.30/Tur.p.54).

Note: Abu bin Edhem's full name was Abu Ishaq Ibrahim bn. Edhem (d.A.D.782) a crown prince of Belkh, who abandoned his Kingdome for God like Buddha. He is also founder of Edhemiye sect. He once said, "If you want to be loved by God, then empty your heart of this world and also of the other world. Just love God".

3- The story: How Ibrahim Edhem abandoned his kingdom of Belkh:

Edhem generously gave away his property and physically obeyed to whatever was required, yet he pondered, "How is it that I cannot attain the spiritual vastness", and he did not know what else to do. One day, he slept away on his throne. While his eyes slept, his soul was wide-awake. The royal guards played drums and flutes harshly, making a huge noise. Edhem thought, "What kind of enemy are they trying to keep away from me when my enemy (ego) is lying beside me. We all are helpless and only God's assistance can protect us". His mind was preoccupied with these ideas and he raised and lowered his head on the pillow, how can lovers sleep? All of a sudden he heard strong footsteps on the roof of his palace as if some persons were walking here and there. Now, the king began to think, "What has happened to the guards? Can't they see these people running on the roof?" He was filled with awe and he had lost the power to call for the guards. Just then, someone peeped down the roof and asked Edhem, "Who are you settled downed on the throne?" "I am the king and who are you on the roof?" said the king. The stranger said, "We have lost some camels and we are looking for them". Now, the king said, "You really mad!" The man replied, "Actually you are mad". The king said, "Is this the right place looking for the camels?" "Well do people look for God by sitting on the throne?" After this no one saw Edhem and many souls left with him. If you don't give yourself up to a thing totally, that thing looks hard and difficult (Per. p 27 Tur. p.49-50)

4- Love the poor and the helpless in order to gain God's love:

It is said in the Koran, "Give God a generous loan" (73/20). What does God really need? Once God said to Moses, "I am hungry, will you feed me? If I come at the door of your house, how will you treat me?" Moses said, "How can this be possible because you are above all needs?" But God said again, "Shall you feed me, if I come at your door, I am really hungry? Leave this discussion; go home and prepare the food for me. I will come tomorrow." Moses had dishes prepared early in the morning for God. Moses noticed that all was ready except water. Just then a dervish appeared and begged for some food in the name of God. Moses having received him handed two jars to him and said, "Go and fetch some water". The dervish replied, "I am at your service, sir". When the dervish brought the water Moses gave him the food. The dervish thanked Moses and left the house. Well, how can a man like Moses be mistaken in this way although he was told to write down the Old Testament in Gold, and he knew chemistry? As the day passed, Moses waited and waited. Desperately, he gave the food to his neighbors and began to think about the secret of the matter. When a suitable time arrived, Moses asked God, "My Lord, You promised me to come, but You didn't show up?" God replied, "Well, I did come and you refused to give me food before my fetching two jars of water." The meaning of this story is to teach people to obey God sincerely and give them a wider sense of divine comprehension.(Tur.p. 68/Per.p.39).

5- Love of God softens lustful ego:

Two scholars were arguing and discussing with each other about the secrets of divine knowledge and the stages of saints (God loving-men). One of them said, "The man who is riding the donkey and coming towards me is also God". The other said, "In my opinion the donkey is also God". As a result they fell in the trap of *Jebriya* (the fatalists). It is clear in the statements of Beyazit and others like him that it is not so; and to take their statements in that sense is a matter of shame because they meant something else. Someone said, "What is meant by that? I replied, "For instance, you have overheard our talk and you felt repulsion in your heart. That is the kind of curtain I am alluding to. They (the saints) are close to *hulul* (incarnation of God). That is, the words uttered by them like those of Hallaj (see here), who said, "God incarnates in our body", are above your comprehension because you are still filled with lust and desires. I don't want to discuss again about lust for I have already said about it. The feeling of love kills lust and worldly desires; and when that divine love comes into an action all the beauty of the world is nothing more than a wall brick. Whenever God's lover hears or reads some words of wisdom, his love comes into action. Finally, the love curtains of light appear as Muhammad said, "God has seventy (many) curtains of light". Now that you are drowned in lust, how can you talk about the light, and even if you do that will be all lust and show. That Sufi Amad is drunk most of the time and shakes his head, which is also show. What show has to do with the light of God? (Tur.p.69/ Per.p.40).

6- God is visible to some:

If anyone wraps up a diamond in a black handkerchief and covers it with ten coverings and then hides it under the sleeve of his robe, it becomes invisible to many, which is no matter of surprise. Similarly, Seyyid (Burhaneddin, Rumi's first teacher) when he received the scent and beauty of his soul, he could not see his soul openly as seeing the soul is another stage, which should be preferred. That is the stage where you can see God in this world and hereafter. The diamond (mentioned above) may be covered up, yet it has such a strong light that leaks out. Those who are perfect in vision can detect it; and it is no matter of surprise. However, it is a matter of surprise if someone fails to see the diamond when it is exposed on a palm. Such a person will not understand the teachings of Socrat, Akhwan-i Safa and other philosophers. The same person will not understand Muhammad or his followers (who are like his children); and God's Presence. (Per.p.110/Tur.p.170).

Note: Akhwan-i Safa was a group of earlier Muslim philosophers, who wrote 50 treatises on Islamic issues comparing them with the Greek philosophy and pioneers of earlier renaissance of Islam. Their treatises cover Socrates, Platonic, Neo-Platonic and even the Hindu philosophy mingled with the Koranic ideas. They also held that The Old Testament and the New are as important as the Koran. As a matter fact, they believed in all religions that talk about God and His love. They also held that all created beings would return to the same Center ultimately. Their impact on Rumi and Shams is evident.

7- Meaning of Allah-u Akbar (God is Great):

a) When somebody says "Allah-u Akbar" (God is great) then he must think of someone, who is above one's thought and imaginations; and is even beyond the imagination that the prophets of God had, such as Noah, Abraham, Moses or Muhammad (Per.p.205/Tur.p.15).

b) "God is Great" then who is smaller? That is if somebody can imagine in accordance with the capacity of his mind that God is the Creator of heavens, His Center and His Throne, and of His light and Paradise; he can also realize that God is above all conceptions. So, step further in thinking to catch the Reality.

The whole universe is thirsty to meet Him (Almighty). Even the bravest are filled with fear to loose Him. Dears have no profit by looking at His eyes while the lions of the world are captive of His locks (Per.p.216/Tur.II.24).

Note: "locks" = the manifestation of God; "the lions"=lovers of God; "the dear"= unaware of divine love.

8- It is your soul that shall lead you to God:

"God is the Beneficent One, who has established Himself on the *Arsh* (the throne or chair of God that has command over everything) (the Koran 20/4), and the *Hadith* (Prophet's words) says, "He who knows his own self, knows God". There is a treasure concealed in the above Koranic verse, which remains unchanged even if the meanings are exposed. The person who is indulged with his ego, cannot perfect himself or anybody; and "If you speak aloud, then lo! He knows the secret thought and the more concealed" (the Koran 20/7). The place of ego (selfness) is under our feet. You can find Muhammad in Ahd (One-ness), but you cannot find *Ahd* in One-ness (Per.p.315/Tur.II.p.118).

9- God did not create man with two hearts:

It is said in the Koran, "God hasn't made for man two hearts" (33/4); and "Whatever we have (is created) belongs to God" has the same meanings. God never says, *"Analhaq"* ('I am the reality', as said by Hallaj al-Mansur; and no one ever says *"Subahani"* ('I am the Glorious one', as said by Ebu Yazid Bastami). These are the words uttered in the state of bewilderment. God never bewilders over anything. But if a slave (lover) of God says in ecstasy of love "I am Glorious" it can be accepted (Per. p.253/Tur.II.p.60).

Note: "Two hearts in one breast" means God did not create two inconsistent attitudes or having love for this world and for God at the same time.

Halaj al-Mansur (martyred in 919 CE) was executed in Baghdad for saying, "I am the Reality (God)". He was once disciple of Juneyd al-Baghdadi. He emphasized that God is the only source of creation, Muhammad is the eternal light that played role in the creation and all religions belong the same source. He also believed in the descent of God in man (*Hulul*). To get to this stage one has to give up all mundane desires.

Tayfur Abu Yazid al-Bistami (d.874 CE) is the founder of Tayfuriye sect. He believed that God is in every being, and when people worship God, actually God worships Himself. When people asked him, "How did you gain this high spiritual stage?" He would reply, "I killed my egoistic soul like a snake changes its skin; and all of a sudden I found that I was Him". His love for mankind is also unmatchable as he says, "If God gave me permission to intercede for the people of my time, I shall not feel proud, because I will be interceding only for a piece of clay! If God gave a chance to intercede, first of all I would forgive those who gave me harm and those who denied me.

10- Meaning of God's attribute Samad (Eternal and Absolute):

A mad man brought ice and tried to hide it in water. When it did not melt, he asked it, "Why aren't you like us? We (man and God) are also of the same source. Like you, I am the body, and God is the soul or He is the body and I am the soul. Somebody said let me explain you, "Why didn't God say to his prophets: Say that God is One, but He said (in the Koran) to Prophet Muhammad: Say that 'God is one and *Samad*' which is a sensitive matter. 'Samad' means a being that has no stomach for food or any need, while a being with stomach means that it is in need of something. Similarly the number 'one' is the proof of other numbers (Per.p.318/Tur.p.122).

Note: The word *Samad* occurs in the Koranic verse Ihlas (CXII) "He is God, The One and Only; Eternal and Absolute". He is above any physical needs while others are dependent on Him and are temporal in existence. So, as long as we are in physical needs we cannot be dissolved in God.

11- God has maddening scent:

God has His own scent like amber or musk. It emanates before God manifests Himself, which leads to spiritual drunkenness. (Per.p.129/Tur.p.198).

12- Philosophers are lost in search of truth:

There are a few people who believe that God can be seen in dream, or when you are awake. They are imitators; and those who are philosophers and claim to be the truth seekers are more imitators. There are people who are imitators of loving-hearts, piety and even Mohammedan belief. There are other people who claim to be God and speak about Him by imitating saints and vice versa. Such people have their own way of explaining the Koranic verses. For instance, "Say though the sea became ink for the words of my Lord, verily the sea will be used up to explain what He is" (18/108). Here they say 'He' has double meaning: God Himself and His Reality. Some, however, say that the personal pronoun 'He' is used here by God for modesty. In this sense, the discussion becomes more interesting. To use third person in one's absence is a scandal while to use in one's presence is rudeness and indecent. A person who talks about someone has these possibilities: the person under discussion is absent, in that case his speech is a scandal or the person is present then it is insolence. It is insolence to talk about a person in abundance in his own presence. If a devotee of a Sultan out praises him saying "This sultan did this, did that.." etc. is insolence and the devotee is not a true one. Slander is a great sin. It is as big a sin as these: false accusation, murder and cruelty, which cannot be forgiven. One has to suffer for them unless the Sultan shares one's secrets (Tur.II p.48/Per.p.242).

13- God is God:

All created beings cannot be God, even Muhammad or others. My disciple came and said, "Sorry I couldn't cook anything today". I said, "Well, I don't want anything to be cooked by you, but it will be better that you cooked yourself (become more mature in spiritual matters)". He said again, "How can I be more mature?" On this I replied, "What kind of a disciple are you that you don't understand symbols?". He answered, "Well, if the symbols and allusions were not misleading, there would be no confliction among the Islamic scholars on the sentences and allusions of the jurisdiction and interpretations. They would know one and the same meaning". Upon this I replied, "How can (learned) Islamic scholars contradict on a subject? It is the production of your own assumption and prejudice that you see duality in them. If Abu Hanife had ever met with Imam-i Shafi, he would have kissed his eyes leaving all their differences aside. How can Godly men oppose God? How can such opposition be possible? You see the contradiction, sacrifice your (ego) and you will see no difference". He asked further, "How can I get rid of the problem of sacrifice?" I said, "Do sacrifice your selfness so that you may become free". We say "God is Great" in prayers to sacrifice our active ego and to gain God's contentment. God has to be Great because when you feel proud of your own being, you should say so and surrender to Him. Now, tell me how long will you carry idols under your arms and come to prayers with them? You say, "God is Great" yet you carry the idols under your arms like the infidel and hypocrite. (Tur.II.157/ Per.p.357).

14- Don't give heart to mortal things:

God's ocean of mercy is always active. Whatever you ask from Him, He gives you. All worship for something. Some worship for beauty, while others worship for gold and grandeur, and they say, "This is our God". They never say, "We don't love the things that set down (like the sun or stars)" as Prophet Abraham said (the Koran 6/76). Where is the man who could show courage of uttering those words like Abraham? The secret of this lies in the other heaven because there are other stars and planets in that world (which do not set, they are immortal). When you pass these physical attachments, you discover that these things are not eternal. When imaginations break through the esoteric world, divine light appears and says Abraham's words: Lo! I have turned my face towards Him, who created the heavens and the earth (the Koran 6/79); and when I am sick he gives me health (26/79). In this verse although personal sickness of Abraham is referred to, but it teaches us "God we have wronged ourselves" (words of Eve and Adam 7/23). In other words, "I am sick and my health comes from God". Here when selfness is denied, divine power is proved (Tur.p.160/ Per.p.360).

15- Some speak about God without knowing much about Him:

A priest preaches people, gives them hints about the goal and shows them a way to God, but an imperfect Sheikh or poet speaks about the path of God and is embarrassed in the presence of a wise man, like the man in this story: A man was talking about fish while the other stopped him and said, "You know nothing about fish. Why do you try to tell about something that you don't know?" The man replied, "That's what you think, I know what fish is like". The other man said, "Alright if you really know then explain". The man replied, "The sign of fish is that it has two horns like camel". "Well, I was sure you didn't know about fish and now by your explanation I understand that you don't know the difference between a cow and a camel" (Per.p.21).

16- Prophets, unlike dervishes, have to contact people:

The Prophet Muhammad (p.h.) once said, "There is a time when no existent or angel can come between me and God". I asked a sheikh "Is this state regular or irregular?" The silly sheikh said, "It is not regular but occasional". I added, "A dervish prayed for Muhammad:

'May God grant you plurality!' Upon this Muhammad stopped him and said, "Don't ask for plurality; ask for individuality because I am fed up with associating with the public" (Tur II.p.138/Per.p.337).

Note: Muhammad said so because he preferred to be with God more than with the common folk.

17- Change vengeance into mercy:

If a vengeful man looks at a merciful man with the intention of vengeance, he feels nothing but revenge. This slave of God (Shams) once said to an infidel, "You are the slave of God and so am I, but you are born out of revenge and I am of His mercy. Mercy is superior to vengeance. So, give it up for the taste of mercy, which is far better (Tur.p.59/Per.p.33).

18- Look up to God with love:

One should look at a beloved with loving eyes. It is said in the Koran: "And God loves them". The problem is that some don't look at God with love. They try to look at

Him through knowledge, philosophy or Gnosticism, while to look at Him with love is a different thing (Tur.71/Per.42).

19- God is covered behind many curtains of light:

God has many curtains of light and darkness that do not undo the knots of hopes even if one keeps on studying (books) for ages. No one can fully comprehend Him; and studying books will be of no assistance in this matter. Readings of books will be like loading donkey's back with books. What benefit will donkey get out of those loads? If you say something and your like-tempered gives no attention to your talk, and fails to feel like you there is no use of talking to him. Nevertheless, you need a person who can understand you and what you say; otherwise it is useless to talk to him. Now, if someone speaks to you and you try to understand him according to your knowledge and philosophy, can you really enjoy his speech? There are many who spend ages together and yet they fail to understand each other. However, if you can find someone of your taste, you can regard yourself lucky (Per.103/Tur.161).

Note: To understand God, one needs to pass through His curtains, and be close to His wisdom.

20- Those that have divine knowledge (Ilm-i Ledun) are of two kinds:

Those over whom knowledge passes like a flood, they are the travelers of knowledge. Only a few of them can tell the secrets. They have spiritual beauty manifest on their faces. Then there are those whose faces read no spiritual signs, yet many prophets and friends of God yearn to meet them and see their faces. Someone may object to this idea by saying "How can these people be close or above prophets?" The answer is that they believe in (love of) God by birth and that is their target of life. There are people who believe whole-heartedly in the Koran and the words of Muhammad and that are their target. What else can be expected from them? If they begin to think like the former people, then where shall they end up? They are stuck while God's world is extremely wide and endless (Per.122/Tur.188).

21- The meaning of Faqr (asceticism):

There are many (thousands) meanings of: "If one accomplishes the stage of asceticism, he becomes God". It actually means that when you accomplish the stage of asceticism, God appears to you and you find Him and see Him, but it does not mean that you become God. In other words, if you complete the stage of Faqr, you might meet with God; and if you don't accept my interpretation, you may commit blasphemy and there no difference between you or a Christian. As a matter of fact Jesus had lighter soul than Khalaj al-Mansur or Bayazid- i Bastami. So if a Christian says that Christ is the Son of God then why should one blame him? Consequently, the meaning of "If you accomplish faqr you find God" will come to mean that "If one kills one's nafs (sensual desires or ego) he gets rid of Satan, and being purified he may meet with God. This meeting does not mean that you meet with God directly but it means you have discovered a way to Him; and you realize that you have entered God's path and not met with Him. Now, if you take otherwise, you loose your way to Him and your evil desires become stronger. He who cannot differentiate between the light of divine path and the light of God Himself is mislead and falls into darkness (Per.128 / Tur.197).

22- Divine guidance is above self-learning:

There is no doubt that the creation of this world has an aim and reason; and there must be a lucky person for whom this palace has been decorated while the rest of people are his servants and subject. Whatever is created is created for him and he is not created for it. For example, a rich man has a special guest and he has built a grand palace for him to stay and he himself lives somewhere else. There are people who search for the palace. However, not all the seekers have the scent of the way to the palace unless the Host helps them. Although some seekers leave this world and knowledge aside, and ignore the learned that are weaker than them, they cannot reach the goal they are thirsty for, because the divine knowledge is not available by means of labor. One may try to find it by studying the sky and the earth, yet it has no avail. He will be left out in darkness and will be deserted. Nevertheless, if he finds a lover of God, he can reach his aim. As a matter of fact, God loving man is also in search of that man. Now, if I say "I am that man and Rumi had fallen behind" it will not be incorrect to say that he is lucky to reach his goal by finding me (Per.137/Tur.208).

23- The stage of istighraq (absorption):

The prophet Muhammad was absorbed in himself because action needs sincerity and to serve others also needs sincerity that requires absorption in God. When the

Prophet discovered that not all could attain deep absorption and find way to real action, he ordered for five time prayers, fasting and Haj in order not to be deprived of absorption. Those who are already absorbed in the Divine Ocean are perfect persons and free from formalities. However, it is possible for the conventional to obtain absorption by means of ritual prayers; and if they fail to do so, then what is the use of hunger (fasting) and obedience to God? What is the profit of these physical pains caused by remembering God (Zikr) and prayers? (Per.153-154)

Note: 'Istighraq' is a Sufi term, which means to be submerged in the Divine Ocean of Unity (see Farhang-i Lughat-i Istilahat).

24- Finding God makes you eternal:

Of course five time prayers are obligatory in Islam and one can offer them openly. You can offer such obligatory prayers openly even if your path of belief is different. At night you may leave your wife asleep, amuse your son with dry grapes and your daughter with walnuts and go to prayers until dawn. This is all right because Muhammad's religion is so. You may go to a mosque upon a call (Ezan) and pray in privacy. If you miss your meditation because of the call, you have to return to God once again. That is the right thing to do. If you do so you get rid of fear of death and worries, which will decorate you with the attributes of God. Then you will understand the eternal liveliness greatness of Rumi. If death sees you from a distance, it will die because you have gained divine life. You can walk silently being unnoticed on this path (Tur.223).

SHAMS and RUMI

Rumi has a charming face, and I have a nice face as well as a bad face. Rumi had seen my nice face but not the bad one. Now I don't want to be hypocrite, I can show my bad face to him so that he may see my wholeness: My good side and my bad side (Per.20/Tur.40).

One who enters my company gives up other's companies because he finds them insipid. Actually, he fails to converse with others (Per.20/Tur.40).

When I was a child, I had reached a strange stage, which no one knew, including my father. Once my father said to me "Son are you mad and what is the matter with you? You had no special training or anything like that (to follow the Sufi path)". I said to my father, "Listen to me, our situation is like this: An egg of duck is brooded under a hen, and a chick has been hatched. When it grows a bit, it can jump into water without hesitance while the hen, being a terrestrial bird, fails to do it. We are just like that. Dear father! My home is in the sea in which I want to swim like the sea birds. If you are like me then come along or go with the domestic fowls". He said (my father):

If you treat a friend like that, how will you treat your enemy? (Per.22/ Tur. 42).

I have no interest in common people, and I haven't come for them. I choose those who lead others to God (Per.25/Tur.47).

Once people said, "Rumi has freed himself from the worldly desires, while Shams has not". He (Rumi) said, "Probably, it is because you don't like Shams, if you did, you would not find him despicable and desirous:

A loving-eye does not find faults,
While an angry eye sees all the faults (Per.38/Tur.66).

Someone came and said, "Tell me some secrets". I said, "I cannot tell you any secrets. I tell secrets to only those in whom I see myself. Now, I don't see myself in you, I see others in you" (Per42/Tur.71).

Rumi is a diver and I (Shams of Tabriz, May God perpetuate His Blessings on me) am a merchant; and the pearl lies between us. Some one said, "It is said that the way to the pearl is between you, then let us find our way through that also". I said, "Yes, but I am asking nothing from you. Come here humbly and ask what the way that leads to God is?" Then someone asked humbly, "Which way leads to God?" I replied, "This the way of God, however you have to pass over a bridge while going to Aksaray (a town in Turkey) as it is said in the Koran: 'Fight for God with their wealth and their lives' (the full verse is: Those who have believed and have left their homes and fought for God's cause with their wealth and lives are of much greater worth in God's sight 9/20). So they have to sacrifice their wealth first, and there are many other things to be done. There is no other way to Aksaray, and when you get there you come to wild valleys and lose your way. You loose your way and come across wolves that may attack you. Now what shall you do and give in return? Now, tell me what is your intention? If you have any problem let me know so that I may solve it and make your life easier. I know ways better than you. I am talking about the pearl but you do not give me more than a penny! Should I be hypocritical or straightforward? Rumi is the moon, normal eyes cannot see my sun-like body but they can see the moon; because of the strong light people cannot see the sun directly. Even the moon cannot reach the sun, but the sun can reach the moon. As is said in the Koran: 'Visions do not comprehend Him, but He comprehends all the visions' 6/103. (Per.48/ Tur.81).

God has rewarded, with His mercy, that I can take care of many jobs at a time. God has full power and control over everything. Some saints are quick at showing that they are powerful, actually they are not so while others are more modest in this matter although they are powerful and active; and every thing happens in accordance with their will and they wait until claimants give up (Per.50/ Tur.83).

I have such a character that I pray even for the Jews saying "May God show them the right path!" Those who swear me I pray for them and say, "May God give them something better and more pleasing than the swearing so that they begin to pray to God and be directed to the Divine World. Some people discuss about me asking, "Is Shams a friend of God (*Wali)* or not?" Whether I am or not it is none of their business. It is like this story: Once they said to Juha (Nasreddin) "Look sir some people are taking trays of sweets". Juha said, "It is none of my business". They said again "They are taking them to your house". This time Juha replied, "Then it is none of your business!"

This is the reason that keeps me away from mixing up with the common folk. I love many sages secretly and I don't tell this to anyone. To my experience, there is a kind of love that never fades away and many don't know the value of such love. My love for Rumi never abated, on the contrary it increased. I cannot tell the truth, and if I do, they (people) will send me away. If I ever told them the whole truth, they will expel me from this town (Per.50/ Tur. 84).

Rumi is a Godly man (a saint) therefore one should talk to him about serious matters. Recently, we have been talking about love of God, but in the presence of normal people we should talk about the fear of God (Per.58/Tur.95).

I was sitting somewhere in the corner of a caravansary when someone asked me, "Will you come to the *Khangah* (convent)?"

"I don't see myself worthy of that Khangah" said I, and continued, "Khangahs are made for those who do not worry for cooking food and doing anything else. Their time is precious for them. I am not that kind of person." "Well" he said, "Won't you come with me to the Med rise then?" I replied, "I don't like to discuss matters. If I understand the deeper meanings of the words, then why should I discuss further? When I discuss the matter in my own way, they laugh at me, and they think that I am infidel. I am a poor (humble) person, therefore I deserve this corner of Caravansray only"(Per.62/Tur.101).

My soul was stationed at a stage where I could go no further, and I thought that was the end of the road. He (God) lifted me up to a higher stage; and due to His Mercy and Clemency, He lead me further. Now, when I say something to others, you can take out of it what you need (Per.102/Tur.159).

I swear, no one can equal Rumi in knowledge and poetry.

No one can be as shrewd and quick at answering to questions as he is, not even Moses (Per.117/Tur.180).

People like Rumi even when he speaks in his normal mood, although there is lack of eloquence in his speech, people like it. But when he warms up in conversation his real value appears and all the young and old begin to appreciate him being lured to love. They know that Rumi bears my company, and which words belong to me and which don't. This is how Rumi is. I too have a situation of my own. I don't care for what people say or think about us. It may appear rather egoistic but we both agree to that. I have yet to say many things, and I am afraid I can't manage it and try to summarize my speech. Therefore, I shun details and but I don't want to go astray and I plea my words not to mislead me (Tur.182).

13. I said to them openly that they would fail to understand my speech. You (Rumi) say to them that I have no ordinance from God that I should explain to them in simple words about what I say. I tell the truth which is heavy for them to comprehend, and when I explain things with their opposite examples, they are covered up under thick layers and become more concealed. Rumi avoids such method while explaining Divine Matters. I have discussed these matters with him exclusively to bring

them all to light. Now, when they listen to him, they accept his ideas and leave the spot with submission like dervishes (Per. 128/Tur.196).

14. I have not brought my spiritual state form Aksaray or Kaymaz Caravansary, and I hold no such opinion. I have brought it from Aleppo and from many other places. I am here (in Konya) as an old man in this severe winter. I wouldn't be here if you did not show me obedience and closeness (Per.129/Tur.198).

15. I asked myself, "What do I have to do with drinking and sleeping if my God, who has created me like this, does not speak to me and does not answer to what I ask Him by any source. I have come to this world to drink the wine of blindness (wine of Divine Reality) and when I have done this I should be able to talk to Him and listen to Him directly; and after drinking that wine, and being aware of why I am here and where I shall go; I could go to sleep. The spiritual wine shall also teach me about how I can obtain full freedom and what shall be my end. I had this purpose ever since my childhood, so I turned my attention to the principles of that goal. My situation is like this: Suppose that a mother has an only lad in this world and he is handsome and attractive. One day, he burns his hand and the mother begins to worry to find out a way to save him (from the fire). Similarly, scent of God saved me and protected me (Per.130/Tur.199, Mak.M. 734).

I like the man who swears me, and the one who praises me gives me no pleasure, because praises cannot be denied later. Well! The hypocrite is worst than the infidel as the Koran says, "Lo! The hypocrites will be in the lowest depth of Hell 4/144 (Per.149).

My ego is so trained that if you put many deserts and Kebabs in front of me, I will refuse them despite of my hunger. I do not look at such things although many adore them. It is better to feed myself with barley bread to quench my hunger on time than to feed it with rich foods when I am not hungry (Tur.227; Mak.M. 718).

Everybody knows that even a non-living creature cannot tolerate me more than seven months at a *Tekke* (Sufi Sanctuary). People go mad when they listen to me at Medrises, yet why should I make a wise man mad? Then there will be left no one to understand me. However, I may or may not be a Sufi but this threshold (*Dergah*) is full of people who don't worry about buying food or cooking. Even non-living objects have desires to meet each other when separated, but their sounds are unheard as the Koran says, ".... And there is not a thing but hymns His praise but ye don't understand" 17/ 44 (Tur. 230).

I have such a feverish mood that many can't understand it. However, those who listen to my words may be healed. When my words find roots among public, they will become more powerful (Tur.290; Mak.M. 766).

Rumi speaks about esoteric matters, and when he does so he does not care whether others benefit out of it or not. However my situation is different. I have spiritual inspirations ever since my childhood. Thus, if I train someone, he can get rid of self-centeredness and steps onwards (Tur.291; Mak.M. 767).

I took some soup yesterday and ate nothing else. If I did not abstain from food I would be sick now. My body has been purified. I keep it healthy by the fire of abstinence and feel sorry when I don't do so. God keeps my heart ready for diet and I never miss it (Tur.293; Mak.M.768).

I have much pain (due to traveling) and haven't recovered from the fatigueness for the last two years. I have returned to Konya by bearing all the pains and sufferings once again. It is your love that has brought me here; otherwise I wouldn't come to Konya even if they (people) filled the town with gold. It has not been possible for me to abandon a man of God (Rumi) for sake of a child (probably Rumi's son who was against him). (Tur. 297).

Traveling is hard for me. If I leave this time, don't do as you did before. Presently, I cannot travel. I can't go even as far as Aksaray. May be I can stay here in a corner where there is less trouble. For the last two years, I have lost my energy to travel. I am tired of the discomfort caused by the journey. If there were no private meetings and confidential conversations between us, I would leave this city again, and you would not stop me as before. He (probably Rumi's son) will join us again and will promise not to act against our will or possibly he may misunderstand our speeches. However, if he acts according to my advice each of them (sons) will turn into angels (Tur. 298).

I was like a pearl (diamond) fallen in litter. Now, I think I am out of that, and I am shaking hands with a

Muslim brother (most probably Rumi). The more I shake my hands with him, the more my sins decrease. Well then this the time to act and do something. "O Muslims come on, move on so that we also move.." (Tur.307).

My words are in me. Anyone who wants to hear my words will have to enter my inner world, but there is a doorkeeper of that world who should be visited first (Tur.310;Mak.M 322).

Rumi writes with the light of God. He may find something or he may not. We must run our eyes on his words so that we may understand them clearly. I conceive that I have been waiting to be inspired by God. May He put everything in order to make them easy for my conception! In the man, who was offering his prayers, I could not see his inner self clearly. Sometimes it happens that I loose Divine inspiration and anger takes over me. Again I transfer from non-existence to existence, which I find very strange and funny. One has to be concentrate enough at such states because you observe strange things, and you pass from one stage to another. When you look up you have a new state, and when you look down you see another (Tur.311; Mak.M 322).

Anyone who happens to see us will become Muslim of Muslims (a strong Muslim) or infidel of infidels because he will look and judge us outwardly; and will not be able to probe into our esoteric world. Some people looking at us generally find us outwardly imperfect in regular prayers and being at a high spiritual stage, they think, we don't need them. They also quit the prayers, but they loose their bond with the other world (by doing that). (Tur.233).

Every four day I feel a bit lazy and sleepy, and soon this state comes to an end. That time I can hardly take a single morsel of food. People ask me, "What is the matter with you?" This is my reply to them, "Nothing serious, I am mad for Someone (God) for whom I can tear my clothes, and if I visit you I can tear your clothes too". Then they ask me, "Why don't you eat anything?" My reply is, "I don't eat anything today or tomorrow or even after that day". What value has a countryman? Even my father was a stranger to me, and I was a stranger in my own country. I was afraid of my father. I thought that he would fall on me and hit me and send me away from his house even when he spoke in a normal tone. I would say to me, "If my spiritual being was born of him, then it should be his child that would flourish and grow up under his guidance to maturity. No, I was a like a goose egg bred by a hen" (Tur. 234).

Sometime Rumi and I miss a ritual prayer because of some job and we don't do it on purpose. We make up the prayers secretly. In addition, if I miss Juma (Friday) prayers, I feel upset. I feel unhappy to fail to join the spiritual values of the Juma prayers with the spiritual values I already posses (Tur. 238; Mak. M. 742).

If someone claims to love someone really, he/she has to prove it. The proof can be to give some of possession or donation. Just like Rumi, who loved me and gave me protection and gifts when I came to Konya. I accept these all as God's grace (Tur. 262).

I feel no botheration if I leave Rumi or be with him. My loving a thing or despising it depends on my nature. It is because of this that some can't live with me (Tur.264; Mak.M 757).

However, it is a matter of great pleasure to be with you but if I go to Tabriz, people will give a house, property and a respectful job. Nevertheless, I enjoy staying here (Tur. 264).

When Rumi wants to hear something, I understand that he and I have an intention to speak; and when I find him modest, I begin to tell a story and nothing else (Tur.268).

Ever since I have left my country, I haven't found a real Sheikh. Rumi deserves to be a Sheikh but he does not give a robe until someone insists him to do so. However, giving a robe in this way is not as suitable as Rumi should tell someone to be a disciple and then give him a robe, which he never does (Tur. 271; Mak.M 756).

Note: When a Sheikh becomes pleased with his disciple, he gives him his own robe (*Khırqa*). The robe has two meanings: either it is given to a disciple who has been accepted to the sect or it is a sign that he will represent the Sheikh. There are many other kinds of robes: 1-Robes of honor 2- Robes of repentance 3- Robe of blessing etc.

I saw a Sheikh who glared at me first, and then bowed, lowered his head, prostrated and began to role on the ground beating his head with his shoes. I said, "The man who has seen the elephant in full deserves this kind of show. Although a part of that animal may also surprise a person, but it cannot give the surprise that the full elephant can ("Elephant" is a reference to the story of the blind and the elephant and stands for full manifestation of God) (Per. 305/ Tur II.109).

How nice was the recitation of the Kuran in Persian and how nice was the inspiration provided by it! I happened to hear a sound of the *Chang* (a kind of harp) when I was passing through a street. Someone said that there was Sema being performed. The Chang created a spiritual aura. All of a sudden these words came out of my mouth: "Don't hear, don't see", at that moment my ears stopped hearing for some it is a miracle and for some it may be strange. First, I would not sit among theologians instead I would join dervishes because I thought theologians are unaware of the states of dervishes. When I came to know what dervish is and what theologian is, I began to be among theologians because they suffer for learning while the dervish only claim to be a dervish, and certainly it is difficult to be a real dervish or Sufi (Per. 306/Tur.109).

"Soon shall you see when the dust settles down,
What you are riding on, on donkey or a horse."

Many times this dust cleaned off and we saw that we were riding on an Arabian horse. The human body is manifest in this universe while the other world is manifest in his body (Per.322/Tur 125).

I saw all the houses and the city revolve around that miraculous, inexplicable light. I looked up I saw no roof of the house. In that state my father uttered, "Oh my son" and tears shed out of his eyes like two bloody streams. In this situation he wanted to say more, but no words uttered out of his mouth. He left the spot filled with sorrow (Per.323/Tur.127).

I have nothing to do with worries because my selfness has become non-existent and all worries have ended up. My body is filled with joy. Now, why should I worry with the exoteric displeasures? I have thrown away all worries out of my house by means of eliminating swearing and reproaching and answering to the questions as Prophet Muhammad had once said, "We have finished the small war and now we have to wage a greater war (with our selfness and ego)" (Per. 324/Tur.127).

You (Rumi) can be one of them (the people round you) or they can belong to you. But I belong to none. They have beards and I don't have any. Moreover, I am here only for Rumi. He kept himself away from me (due to hesitance) and I requested him to arrange a private meeting with me for two or three days. He did so. The sun provides light to the whole world. Rumi saw the light coming out of my mouth concealed under the darkness of my words. The sun has its back towards the people and its face to the sky, and the light of earth and sky is because of the sun. The face of the sun is also towards Rumi, and his face is towards the sun (Per.113/ Tur. 174).

Presently there is no match of Rumi in any part of the world in arts, such as doctrines, jurisprudence, grammar and logic. He can speak with the learned emphatically, rhetorically and impressively. If he is in the mood and has no worries, and the topic is of great interest, he can be very influential. If I try to learn many years the wisdom of this physical world, I cannot reach his level. He is unaware of his talents. When he listens to me, I feel embarrassed to say so; he sits in my presence like a two years old child or like a new Muslim, who knows a little about Islam. One day, I was speaking about the other world when he said, "I have never heard anything like that ever since I have had these ears" (Per.124/Tur.192; Mak.M. 735).

I have no other desire left. You are reading from your pages. Read from the pages of your Beloved, that will be more useful. You suffer these worries because you read all this out of your own pages, but you should read the words of your Friend. That idea of Beloved is born by means of divine knowledge and learning; and after that achievement, you come across another kind of knowledge that has different vast ideas (closer to God). However, there is another short cut to God, which has become notorious. We have to find a new name for that (Per. 126/Tur. 194).

Greater attention is needed to understand what Rumi says, because his speech is full of jests and puns like magic. Suppose that there are two persons sitting side by side and they both have bright wide-open eyes that are not affected by any pain or dust. One sees everything while the other sees next to nothing. Yes, God loving people do not speak for teaching, but one can take a good lesson out of their speeches. A wise man once said, "He is full of his own knowledge and art like a jar full of brackish water. Empty that water so that one may refill it with fresh water" (Per. 143/Tur.215).

Now, I want to talk about the scandal that has hurt Rumi. Some say that Shams copy words of Rumi. Well I make use of his talk as far as some hints are concerned. His hints refer to me and not you. Don't you realize that he found me alone and gave me shelter and peace of mind? When he chooses someone as a friend, he never gives up. All what he dreams at night becomes true in the morning and its impact continues until noon. I tried to stop it from becoming a routine for Rumi (Tur.229)

I swear, it is a great delight to see Rumi's face. Anyone who wants to see Prophet Muhammad's face should come and see Rumi, and bow to him humbly like grass to the blowing wind; and those who do not want to do so they are welcome to live as they wish. But he, who is able to discover Rumi, is lucky. I have found him once in my life and I am happy. If you have some doubts about belief, he can free you from them by showing short cuts (Tur.250).

I don't remember what day it was. Rumi would have been cross with me because of what I said (but he wasn't). As a matter of fact, I would have avoided saying what could hinder our friendship. Rumi was modest as usual and he did not mind what I uttered, and he said, "I will do what is essential". Well the modesty he showed is a common thing among Sheikhs. It is the virtue that they must posses and it will continue to live, and is as eternal as God (Tur.252).

I pleaded to God. "My Lord! Show me your friends and let me bear their company". In my dream they said, "We shall show you a friend of God". I asked, "Where is that friend of God?" Next night they told me the friend was in Anatolia. Later I saw another dream and this time I was told that the time hadn't come yet to meet with him (Tur.274).

Samarqand is a beautiful city. There are many other beautiful places in the world hereafter that you cannot see here in this world. The actual beauty of this world is on the other side. Rumi says that he does not like my absence, but I have to be away. I walk around every where and sit in every shop. Rumi has a dignified personality, therefore I can't make him go from shop to shop and visit every place like that because he is a Mufti of the town. I cannot take him to a common place like a stoke hole of a Turkish bath and let people see us together (Tur. 276).

I dreamt that Rumi and I were reciting this verse, "Everything will come to an end, except God's face" (28/88). It means that everything (the whole phenomenal world) will perish except the face of the Beloved: "Many lovers mad and out of their minds, come to Your gate crying and shedding tears". "Lantarani" (Thou canst see Me 7/143) is a clear address to Moses, but you cannot see God with these sensual eyes because He is very bright. Else where in the Koran is said, "Eyes cannot see Him, but He can see the eyes" which is above the previous verse in meaning. The verse "Thou canst see Me, but look on the mountain 77/143" Mountain here symbolizes your own body (Tur.279).

Now I must go and see Rumi. He has come to this world neither for any need nor to complete any sign. As a matter of fact, he has no sign to offer of the Beloved, who has no sign in this world. Any visible sign is for a seeker and not for the person (being) sought. These words belong to the (ordinary) seeker. The real seeker has a light that shines for the One sought. Through this light he is able to recognize the happy good people and the unhappy miserable people or the bad natured. The God-seeker has come to this world for watching. Meanwhile some are able to have contact with the Sought. Then there are those who see the God-seekers and become restless and uncomfortable. Some may claim, "I am the unique pearl that you are looking for and I have come to this world to watch Him. Now, we have found what we were looking for so let us settle down at this place". The other may say, "This is not the proper place, let's continue". Another one may say, "Let's watch for a few more days". Now we are watching the world with my light every day. Since we have become friends and seekers of God, let's lead the path with my light. The seeker of God may begin to talk early like Jesus, but the Beloved sought gives him permission of talking after forty days and let him see His face after sixteen years or less (Tur.281).

If they had discovered my tendency towards *Shariah* (conventional Islamic way), they would have fed me with grilled cutlets and Tughrak every morning (Tur.283).

It is because of Rumi's love that people can do what my father couldn't do to me. I would have blemished other's fame and honor even if he were prophet with a holy book (Tur. 284).

Note: Shams tolerated all for the sake of Rumi, otherwise being a dervish he would not care for any one.

A person asked Rumi, "What's your opinion about observation in this world?" Rumi said, "If a man discusses about the same subject, he is either backward in observation or he is after only observation. But if the observation is special and should not be discussed with one, then the case is different. Suppose I am not hungry but thirsty, in that case I need water and not meal; and if I have a meal then things will get worse (Tur. 286).

Note: A lover of God should seek for new spiritual observations and should not be stuck.

Rumi's speech is amazing and always need explanation although it suits all situations. As he once said, "First Church is essential because a few can be good Muslims at the beginning". I said, "This is the first time that this idea is put forward"(Tur.290).

Rumi kissed the hands of a man who said, "May God, the Best Creator, bless you". Was his belief damaged? No, because the man spoke on behalf of Caliph Omar and through the light of Muhammad, which the ordinary observers failed to know. As you may notice the words were not his. Caliph Ali would not speak on behalf of Muhammad because God spoke through Muhammad's tongue. Isn't it so even today, what can I say to you or to someone else (who is ignorant of this fact). As long as this world will go on existing, love without sensual desires or lust will continue to live, and nothing can hamper it (Tur. 292).

During my speech, I openly say which words belong to Rumi because we say the same things, and it will never occur to me that he will say something different. Therefore, I have no doubt or discomfort regarding this matter. People apologize and say that when Rumi is with us he is full of joy and he never reproaches us or forces us to do this and do that. He let us free and is modest. If Shams had the similar character, he would not be any hindrance for our coming here. Consequently, I have become a person desired by many, while Rumi has become desires of desires. Neither my father nor my mother had shown interest in me like Rumi. He passes my words to others in the best way. He has done favors to me that I failed to do to him (Tur.294-95).

The aim of creating the two worlds (this world and the hereafter) is to bring two friends together face to face for sake of God without any lust (worldly desires). They do not look for a baker, butcher or bread like me who is so happy in the presence of Rumi (Per. 181/Tur.358).

You need no praise o learned Rumi! You too give up praising him. I am telling this because it does not give him any pleasure. Don't do something that would hurt him instead of making him happy (Per.183/Tur.359).

Rumi was lost in meditation when the imam called for prayers. We all got up to offer the evening prayers. I saw that we all, including the imam, had our backs towards Mecca. When we were trying to finish our prayers, I went backwards to the place where the phlebotomists stood. This idea came to my mind: How strange it is that people are ignorant of the sun that has risen up from the eternity without beginning. Actually what is eternity and beginninglessness? They are the attributes of God that have been invented only yesterday (in the near past). People call the head of the time 'beginninglessness' and the tail of the time 'eternity'. In reality these (human) words mean nothing (Per.284 /Tur II. 88).

When Rumi gets angry with some common people, it is not because of me. I know his character. If he frowns, he does not frown at me because his nature is open to me. He frowns at others for some reason. However, when I am happy, I am not influenced by anyone's happiness, and when I am unhappy I don't want anyone to be affected by it. (Per.356 /Tur.II.155).

I bless you and I am ready to offer you my service. You may have heard this before that I have happened to meet with many dervishes and served them. I have seen the difference between the liars and real dervishes and would not accept them until I really liked them. The *Simurgh* looks down at all birds from a height. He does not care for the courage or timidity of ordinary birds but looks at the talents, bravery and modesty of a falcon. He after that pours his mercy and casts his eyes on the falcon because the other birds cannot fly for hours. Although the falcon cannot see the Simurgh directly, but can feel a secret power in him caused by Simurgh's looks (Per.200).

Note: "Simurgh" is a large imaginary bird like Griffin, which in the mystic language means "a perfect man or friend of God" and "Falcon" means a seeker of Divine Path (Salik).

The populated one-fourth area of this world asks me various questions and gets answers. And whatever difficulties they face they get answers after answers; notes after notes and commentaries after commentaries. However, my explanations have ten answers to one question that no book can provide as Rumi once said, "Ever since I have come to know you, I find books tasteless" (Per.254/Tur.60).

In our presence one cannot be Muslim once. He becomes Muslim and again infidel as sensual desires overtake him. After such changes, he can become perfect. I said, "I have promised a Christian and I must keep my promise". They said, "We are Muslims and he is an infidel, don't go to him". I replied, "Well, he is a secret Muslim because he has surrendered himself to God, but you lack that submission". 'Muslim' means to surrender to God. They further said, "You come to us for submission is achieved by conversation." Upon this I said, "Well I have no obstacle. By the name of God let's try" (Per.286/Tur.II/90).

I don't have any disciples. People requested me to accept them as my disciples and to give them the robe, I fled and they came after me for some distance near a house and laid down their presents there but it was all useless. I have no interest in common people. I choose perfect sheikhs. That day in a meeting, I had a quarrel with a sheikh, and I swore him and hit him in the head. He said nothing. Then there was a man who threw himself down in ecstasy and rubbing his face on the ground he forwarded to me. People around said, "What a pity, this is the oppressed poor fellow who has been waiting (until today) with perseverance". He said, "Leave me alone and don't pity me". People shouted, "He is saying so because of anger". The man whose head I had wounded came forward and began to laugh, shout and roll down on the earth. Now, what these actions have to do with practicing religion? Those who regard these as religious practices are mistaken. What step then they must take? "He who knows himself certainly knows God" (says Muhammad). The commanding soul should change into soul at peace. He who is with God, he has no worries and is free from all fears of the world:

You ask me, "Why your tears have gone rose-red?"
Since you have asked me, let me confess,
Because of your love my heart bleeds,
When broiled it rises and comes out of my eyes

(Per.286)

I was rather reckless and had ignored my prayers since morning and had gone the wrong direction. After a three-day's walk, I climbed up a mountain looking over to a deep valley and a lake. Beyond that lake laid the village and a road leading to it. The place where I stood was so high that the village looked like a ring; and the heaps like small children. To cut a long story short, I put my life in danger. I leapt and threw myself down. People of the village looked at me and thought that I was an animal or a tiger. I slipped downwards until I reached the village. When people saw me they fell down on my feet and thought that I was an angel or the Prophet Khizr. Then they began to talk to each other, "What kind of a creature is this fellow who has been left safe after such a deep fall?" God says in the Koran, "Say o Prophet that God is One" to what does it refer to. It is a modest way of saying, "Say, I am the Only God" which may look a bit harsh. So why should "I am God worthy of praise" be awkward? There is no doubt about this in my heart. You need time to learn such things because you have just sat here with us (Per.330/Tur.133).

Note: "How glorious I am worthy of praise" are the words of Bayazid of Bistam. That is what Shams is referring to.

A group of Sufis had become my friends on the way to Arzinjan. They choose me as their leader. They said, "We shall not camp anywhere or lay a table without your permission. We shall not talk to each other after we have a fight until you allow". Some days had gone by and we had found nothing to eat. It was the watermelon season. A farmer waving his hands shouted at us, "Dervishes, please come here and eat melons for sake of God". I told my companions not to hurry. They complained, "We are hungry and you are also. Let us not deny this miracle". I said to them, "That farm will stay where it is. As a Sufi had bread in his robe and addressing to it he said: You are here anyway, if I can't find anything better I shall eat you. So why to hurry". We rose our hands to our ears as if we were deaf, then we asked, "What do you say, sir?" He insistently said, "Please eat the watermelons". I said to the man, "Under one condition, you will feed the dervishes with whatever you eat." He began to plea me because he had seen the event before in his dream. He continued, "I had collected watermelons for dervishes". Upon that I said, "You should not offer the bad ones and keep the best for yourself, because you want us to eat for God". He became over excited and fell down. The dervishes were entertained for three days with melons and mutton. I said, "This is his good luck" and left them there for three more days; and saying to the man, "This is your good chance" I set out. When I arrived at Erzinjan, I was away from my friends, as no one knew me, I spent good time. We wrestled and had a nice time. When the people came to know me, they began to celebrate the event and gave feasts. Then I tried to go for work as a labor, but no one hired me because I was really feeble. All others went to work. A landlord saw me standing there and sent his slave to ask me why I was standing there idly. I said to the slave, "Have you rented the roads and the city? Please, let me know". Nevertheless, the lord took me to his house and showed me to a nice place. He brought decent food and served it to me and sat in front of me with respect. When I finished my meal he said, "You are always welcome to my house as long as you are in this city. His polite words kept me there. One day when he saw me he said to me, "Now release me from this difficulty. Friendship should not be one sided because there is a way from heart to heart. I have a warm heart for you and think you feel the same way yet you hide it from me. Now tell me why do you do that?" I replied, "Yes, this is my nature. In the beginning I am always rough until I am fully dissolved in my friend in kindness and anger. Kindness has the quality that if you offer it to a five-year-old child he becomes attached to you. The real man is the person, when he finds a leader who has patience and tolerance in face of troubles (like Muhammad), should attach to him. Then he has no fear of perishing; on the contrary, he indulges in thousands of eternities. I saw one person raising his finger. I looked at him and said, "You have been Muslim a thousand times yet you have some sign of infidelity left. If it is not so, then why do you see your helplessness in me?" There was a sheikh present there, who began to advise me, "Talk to people in accordance with their capacity of understanding, and be whimsical to the extent of purity and unity". I replied, "Well you are right, and I have nothing to add since you have courage to advise me" (Per. 333-334/Tur.135-136).

These words of Muhammad sound strange to me, "This world is like a prison for believers" because I haven't seen any prison in this world. I have seen respect, happiness and greatness. If an infidel pours water on my hands (renders some service) he is forgiven and becomes closer to God. How lucky I am! I don't know why I looked down upon myself so far although I was happy and content. Well! I had not discovered myself and now I have found the greatness and respect in me. I had found myself like a diamond fallen in a filthy water drain. I presumed that I had got rid of that filthy drain but, God forbid, it is not like that. I am telling you all this to please you. Now give me your hands to shake, and we shake them with Muslims (who have surrendered to God) in a way that all sins fall away (Per. 368 / Tur.II. 167). Our heart is greater and larger than the skies and the whole universe, then why to contract ourselves with trifle things? How can it be proper for you to confine yourself in a prison while this world is so wide like a large garden; and live like a silk cocoon? It is not fair to linger along with anxieties, groundless suspicions and evil dreams and then plunge into a dark world and sleep away unconsciously. We can make gardens out of prisons; and if we can manage to do it, it will be great! I have never objected Muhammad's words (*Hadis*), but the above lines make me think.

Note: It is believed that once Prophet Muhammad said, "This world is a prison for the believers and Heaven for the infidel" as narrated by Majmual Bahrayin (see p. 268 of Per.).

I say that poison is like an antidote for me. As I have to take it, you are not responsible for that. Be my witness as the Koran says, "Each soul earns its own account, no bearer of burdens can bear the burden of another" (6/164). If I am a sinner, let it be so for I am no more a sinner because Hell hesitates to accommodate me as the Hadis (words of Muhammad) say, "Pass by o thee believers because thy light has extinguished my flames" (Jami al-Saghir, 1/132) (Per 160/ Tur.332).

I am harsh towards those who are my friends, but it may not always be true. It is torture as well as kindness in invitations, but in seclusion (*Khalwat*) there is always kindness (Per.160 /Tur.333).

Tomorrow you have to deliver a lecture as you have opened the door to them. If the door is closed, people will begin to blame and shout. I wish they could make use of your lectures. All have been said to them openly and by allusions, but they behave as if they were never told anything. They fail to understand exoteric as well as esoteric meanings of your lectures. If they don't understand, then what is the use of your lecturing them? Action without knowledge is devastating. After all, what do they do when they spend forty days in *Chilla* (lent) saying, "There is no God other than Allah?" This is not the matter of language, but the matter of heart (Per. 165/Tur.338).

There was a mad man who told secrets. For the sake of test, people would close him in a house and somehow he would come out. One day my father was angry with me and he spoke to people angrily. He came to my father and clenching his fist he said, "Leave this kid alone" and pointed at me. Then he said to me, "Have a nice time". Showing respect to me he left. I never gambled, not because of any obligation but by nature. I could not handle any job, but I would go to sermons regularly wherever they were delivered, because I was created for that job. Like Jesus, who spoke a few words once when he was infant, and then kept silent (Per. 262/Tur.II 69).

Once I was a theologian and I studied Imam-i Shafi's book "al-Tanbih" Now, I don't remember a word of that book. If I face any question some knowledge comes to mind, if not, I let it go. You come to me because it is nicer to be with (old) friends than to be with the young (Per. 243/Tur.II 49).

When I was still a young boy, I would not eat anything due to love of God; and if people talked about eating, I would pull away my hands and turn my head and refuse to eat. When people gave me something to eat, I accepted it because of respect and hid it under my sleeves. Once when I was performing Sema one of my ardent friends got hold of me and took me around as a chick of a bird. I was like a piece of bread snatched away in the hands of a three-day hungry young man who could pierce it in a second. Such was my situation, and my eyes were filled like blood red two bowls (by crying). Just then came a voice; "He is immature leave him alone and let him burn on his own" (Per. 245- 246 / Tur. II.51-52).

A mature Sufi said to his disciple, "Do the Zikr from the belly". I said, "No, do it from the core of your heart and soul" This statement surprised the Sufi. On whom we disclose our real face, can give up the whole world but we avoid doing that. Once Prophet Muhammad said, "To avoid the charms of this deceptive world" in reply to the question, "What is the sign of a true believer?" We have the diamond and if we expose it one can abandon all friends and companions (Per. 283/Tur.II.88).

One day I said to Shams al-Din Khunji, "I want to go and find a job because you don't want to teach me anymore". He said, "Well if I had arranged something, I would have told you". I asked, "What should I do then?" He replied, "Son! What job can you take with this state of ecstatic contemplation and mildness? Your state will surprise even the theologians, who will complain: Look at this man who is working in this job despite his high spiritual position and power!" I said to myself, "He first encourages and then he disappoints me" (Per.299/Tur.103).

Whatever other prophets gained in thousand years, Muhammad gained in a small period of time because he was bestowed with the wisdom of Divine Knowledge. Let's get out and have our moustache shaved, as we are not going to take part in any war where enemies should be frightened. However, our inner enemy is not afraid of any of the hair that turns into a piercing spear. I am not interested in any of these subjects because my soul is at peace for a long time. Someone asked me what is meant by, "He who eats alone is the worst man". It is not easy to explain the real meaning of this to people, as God says in the Koran: "And see your abasement among those who fall down to prostrate (in Sejde)" 26/219. I have joyful tidings within myself, which is strange because there are many who are happy without any tidings; and are ready to refuse even a crown on their heads saying, "All we need is the inner vastness and light. We wish whatever we possessed should have been taken from us in return for the real vastness". When I was a boy they used to ask me, "Why are you upset? Do you need new clothes or what?" I replied "I wish I had no clothes on me at all" (Per. 295 /Tur. II.99).

Note: Literally, the standing and prostrating are the movements carried out in Muslim prayers, which spiritually stand for sincerity, attitude of mind and patience. Prostration is the main symbol of submission to God. That's what Shams refers to here.

There are some people who invite others and tell them to place their heads on their knees to meditate. Somebody, raising his head shouts, "I have seen the highest peak of God's throne and His Seat (*Kursi*)." Meanwhile someone else may claim that his eyes have passed even further to watch the outer space. The other may say, "I see the fish (Pisces) from the Taurus (in the sky) and the angels that are responsible for them". Well! I see only my humbleness among these phenomena and feel like a bird hung up with its legs in the trap of my Beloved (God). Now, to whom should I say hello and call for help? None, for I preferred to be so! I did not ask for a shop but for two mines: the mine of gold and the mine of silver. As a matter fact I asked for none to enjoy full freedom. That is what suits me. Some don't like poverty; they like ego and their own beings. However, it is poverty (the content soul) that leads you to God and protects you from everything else; and the same poverty may take you away from God and lead you to public (which is the physical poverty) (Per. 317 / Tur.II. 120).

One day my Sheikh (probably Abu Bakir Sillabaf) holding an apple in his hand said to his disciple Zeynuddin Kelusi, "I saw God and asked for an apple. He gave one to me. What would you ask for if you saw God? Bayazid of Bistam asked for God from God?" Zeynuddin said, "Well, I will ask for the same". "In this case you are already at the stage of Bayazid" added the Sheikh. I was still a child and the Sheikh asked me the same question. I pointed at him and said, "I would ask for you". He nodded his head and from that moment on I could not speak but my inside was filled with words, phrases and meanings. I had a strange condition, which a child rarely ever has (Tur. 348 /Per.173).

There was a boy in our company, who over heard our speeches. He was wise. He left his parents and became our fan. He offered himself to our service, and because of this his parents were upset and cried. He would not tell me about his parents so that I may send him back. As time passed, gave up worrying about his parents. He was at our beck and call all day long. Now, the parents couldn't say anything. From time to time, I tried to hear what he uttered; and once he recited these lines:

Lovers come swarming through your street and pass by,
They cry and shedding their bloody tears they pass away,
I am like soil, dwelling forever at your threshold,
While others come like wind and then they pass by.
I said to him, "Say again what you uttered".
He refused to reply and passed away at the age of eighteen
(Per.273 /Tur.II.79).

Those dogs call Shahabeddin Suhurwardi 'an infidel'. How can he be an infidel as he is enlightened, especially in the presence of the *shams* (the sun). He changes into the full moon in his presence. Try to understand whatever I say. I am afraid, whatever I say now I say because of anger. Why are you not present when I am angry? I am soft towards my friends but I show myself proud and arrogant to others. God embraces me ten times but I embrace Him only once. Rumi looks for me ten times; I look for him only once (Per.329/Tur.132)

Their (some Sheiks') words are either of Bayazid or Juneyd. We also speak about them, but our words are not insipid like theirs. Those who haven't tasted essence of sugar, they find grape juice sweeter (Per. 329 /Tur. 132).

For a short time, let's go and visit the tavern and see the wretched people. After all God has created those women (prostitutes) even if they are bad or good, let's see them. Let's go to the Church and see people pray. No one has the will (energy) to do what I do. What I do, the imitators don't have to do. It is said that the imitators don't fit anywhere, which is very true (Per.355 /Tur.II.154).

Rumi had no real disciples other than his children (before). He is like a sea in knowledge and virtue, but the point is that people have to listen to him. I know and all know that he is famous for his elegancy in his speech and knowledge (Per 206 /Tur.II 15).

He who is born under the sun rays and belongs to it before birth can open his eyes to the sun, and has the nature of the sun. People say that you speak about the moon or mercy. How can I speak about that? The sun is not aware of the presence of the moon in the universe. The moon and other planets are helpless. People can see the moon with naked eyes, but they can't see the sun and its surrounding, which has no relation with the moon's light (Mak.M.289; Tur.85).

There was a line carved on the gravestone "Life is but for one hour". One hour or two hours or more, well there is always an end of life. It said for the Sufis that they are 'Ibnul Waqt=care only for the moment they are in'. But for us the real time is to be in the service of Rumi. I was like a worm sitting on a goatskin and did not know how to speak rhetorically. May God be pleased with Rumi for he has put all the things in order (Per.191/Tur.370).

Some people believe that ghosts haunt the Turkish baths, however now angels visit this bathhouse because Rumi has changed this place into a Qibla (a direction for worship). Someone said, "This is a wrong idea". The same man did not see Muhammad in his dream for more than two years as he used to do before, and when the Prophet appeared in his dream he asked, "You have been visiting me every Friday in my dreams to quench my thirst. Now I have been like fish out of water and you didn't show up." The Prophet replied. "I have been mourning". The man asked, "For whom?" The answer was "For my believers, who have turned away from the Qibla except seven persons, who came to me,and had the right Qibla". This reality is hidden in this Koranic verse: "None knowth it's (Koran's) allegorical meanings other than God and those who are deeply rooted in knowledge" 3/6 (Per. 204 / Tur. II.13).

Note: The message is that God-loving man's heart is as valuable as the Qibla

On Perfect Men and Saints

Since there are many Satans in the form of men,
Don't give your hand to all hands (Rumi).

Meaning of 'Wilayet':

What is the meaning of *Wilayet* (friendship with God)? It does not mean to govern an army, cities, villages; but it means to govern one's own ego, speech and silence, and to show authority (Qahr) when authority is required and courtesy when courtesy is required (Per. 27 /Tur. 50).

Every created thing is nice:

A lover of God (Sheikh) once noticed people passing by a stinking carcass of a dog blocking their nostrils with fingers, and turning away their faces. When the Sheikh passed by he did not block his nose or turn away his face. People asked him, "What do you see there?" He said, "I see only its white teeth, and look how nice they are!" .. A good man does not complain about anything, his eyes do not look at bad things (Per. 31/Tur.54).

Patience hath its reward:

A man, who is happy when troubles come, is a man who is able to foresee the happy end. Actually, patience means to cast an eye on the end and impatience is the opposite. The first line remains for those who can see the end. A mule asked a camel, "Why do I generally go in the front of the caravan while you come behind us?" The camel replied, "When I come to a slope of a path, I can see what lies further because I have high head, strong determination and bright eyes. By a single look I can see what is behind the slope and under my feet. Here the camel means a Sheikh, who has a perfect sight (Per. 44 /Tur.74).

Any one who has given away his property (in way of God) must have found something better. Similarly, if someone has given up his ego, must have found something better, because a single hair of his body is worth a hundred dinars (golden coins). I say to the wise and intelligent people that they should leave those people alone who are crazy to waste their lives for money and wealth. It is better to find something better than their egos and souls. God says in the Koran, "Surely we shall try you with something of fear and hunger, and loss of wealth and lives and crops; but give good tidings to those who patiently persevere" 2/154 (Per. 240 /Tur.II. 47).

The hidden Sheikhs:

It is a fact that many believe in Sheikhs (saints). They speak about them in sermons and lectures (delivered from pulpits). There are many hidden saints, who are far better than the known ones and are loved by people. Rumi thinks that I am one of such saints. But I believe that if I am not looked for, at least I am a seeker and a strong seeker. A seeker finds his way out of the sought and, as a matter of fact, God is my seeker. No stories have become famous for the sought in books, treatises or in the books of sects. They all talk about the paths of seekers. However, there is one person who throws some light upon the matter: he is Juneyid of Baghdad, who says, "They sell ten cucumbers for one cent then what value do we have in the dust of this world?" This I had explained that day. It was Juneyid's state. Even ten afflicted persons would not reach his purification, which will be a blasphemy for us (to say such things) (Per. 54/Tur.90).

Saints are above scholars:

If it were possible to understand spiritual matters by means of learning and discussing, then it would be fair to carry their clay on heads (respect them to extreme), and Bayazid and Juneyid would serve Fahreddin Razi for many years as his disciples. It is said that Fahreddin had written one thousand five hundred sheets on the Koran (as commentary). Even so, ten thousand Fahreddins cannot reach even the dust of Bayazid's path. The doorknocker ring is out side the house, while the situation of the house is different. Sultan has a private meeting with his special friends of which neither the doorknocker rings nor the window-rings have any knowledge. Thus learning is not enough for the Divine Knowledge, you have to walk and run on the path (Per. 55/Tur.91).

About false saints:

You can notice the false saints narrating stories of others and imitating them. They recite a Hadis (words of Prophet Muhammad) and tell a story or read out some poems of other poets. They have very little of their own. When I say, "Say something of your own", they speak in a spiritual mute language like a wall. Now what can you expect from a wall! (Tur.243).

The Mice and the Cats:

A large number of these sheikhs have been way layers of the Mohammedan religion. They are like the mice that destroy their own house of Islam. But there are also God's cats of the religion that clean the house of these mice. Thousands of these mice have no courage to look at the cats; the fear of the cat will never allow them to congregate. The cats have unity, and if the mice had it, at least some could damage the eyes of a cat during a fight. Consequently, the mice have no such courage. The cats have association, as is said in the Koran: "Do they not see that We have made a sanctuary secure and that men are being snatched away from all around them" 29/67 (Per.154 /Tur.325).

Secret saints with secret hearts:

There are some saints, whose miracles are hidden and they do not disclose their secrets to all. However, he who is all merciful (like a sheik who is always kind to people) is not complete. God is both 'Merciful and Kind' and that is not enough for He is also 'Oppressor'. Actually, there is mercy concealed in God's oppression. Both the attributes suit God, which in reality show up in Him (Per. 156/Tur.327).

Dance of a saint:

A saint's movements or dance is light and gentle. He walks like a leaf floating on the surface of water, although his inside is as heavy as a mountain. May be like many mountains but the outside is like a straw. God is not with me but in my possession (hand). All these attributes that you recite for God such as "Not an atom's weight in earth or in the sky escapes your Lord's Eyes" (10/62) are in my possession too (Per.174 /Tur.349).

Man is a super being:

Human being is above all transient creations and creatures because his wisdom covers God's Seat (*Qursu*) and His Throne (*Arsh*); and whatever is created between the heavens and the earth. His wisdom is above all because God manifests His attribute through human being as is said in the Koran, "Wherever you are you are with God". In order to avoid confusion, God has fixed directions and fields of work so that people may not be distracted. For this reason all deal with some sort of job like chemistry, magic, jewelry, logic, deduction etc. However, some can see the comfort and pleasures of the other world and God's light and God Himself (Tur.311).

Why dervishes (Sufis) suffer in this world:

The Ocean of God's mercy always tends to be effervescent and therefore a Sufi is made to suffer and cry. Unless the clouds of your woes show up, the Ocean of Divine Knowledge does not react. A mother does not nurse a baby with love unless she cries (Per. 176/Tur.351).

The state of raptness (*Istighraq*):

Try not to stay longer in the state of raptness or absorption. Desire higher stages, but some are stuck to this stage, which is not easy to get rid of. If you desire for a higher stage, it is like a jar full of wine, and you fill a glass out of the jar the glass will like to be attached with you asking for more saying, "Let me stay with you for I cannot go elsewhere" although the jar has yet to fill many other glasses. Nevertheless, the jar is weak in front of a stone. If the jar is broken, it looses its content yet the broken pieces remain. The stone does not affect the wine, and it sustains its value as an intercessor. In other words, secret is a menace and requires a distinct reply to those who ask for it. People are never satisfied by silence. They understand only simple statements such as: "Welcome, goodbye, you have honored me etc." Now think what is meant by these Koranic verses: "Haven't you seen how God has spread shadow?" 25/45 and "God is the light of heaven and the earth" 24/35.

Don't hurry in spiritual attainments:

Don't ask me anything my heart has fallen elsewhere again. If you want to make use of my knowledge, be sincere and don't act like Pharaoh, who would say in secret (to God) "You are my God and I am your slave". But in front of his subject he would say, "I am the greatest God of yours" (see the Koran 79/24). Let me take my time in answering to your questions because 'To hurry is the job of Satan'. Those who hurry up (in spiritual matters) see only the outer decoration and forms. Repentance is the character of Adam and his children while to be obstinate is the character of Satan (Per. 177/Tur.352).

On Some Prophets, Scholars and Lovers of God:

Moses and God:

Children (immature persons) read this verse from the Koran "Moses said: Show me (Thyself) that I may see

Thee" God replied, "You cannot see Me (directly), look at that mountain. If it can stand still in its place you can see Me. And when his Lord revealed (His) glory to the mountain, He sent it crashing down. And Moses fell down senseless. And when he woke up he said, "Glory onto Thee....7/142" God was twenty four hours with Moses like the sun that keeps a watch without loosing a smallest amount of its energy (Per. 238/Tur II/45).

Note: Spiritually God is with us but physical senses and eyes cannot see Him fully. An immature man does not believe that God can be seen.

On Nafs (Self Centeredness):

Prophet Muhammad once said, "He who knows his selfness (*Nafs*), knows God". Why didn't he say, "He who knows his intellect (*Aql*) or he who knows his soul (*Ruh*) instead?" someone asked. I said, "Nafs (carnal soul) is the essence of being and should be trained at childhood".

Note: For further information on words: Nafs, Ruh and Aql see A.S.Tritton, Bulettin of the S.O.A.S, University of London, vol. 34/3 1971, p. 491-95.

On Jesus (son of God):

"Say (Muhammad) that God, the Beneficent, has no son and I am the worshipper" says the Koran. Some Christians think that Jesus is God's (physical) son, but not a part separated from Him. However, there are different kinds of interpretations of the word 'birth' for example people say, "These words are born out of his mouth, which is not the kind of real birth (Per. 135 7 Tur.206).

Bayazid of Bistam:

Bayazid saw his selfness fat and asked it, "Why are you so fat?" "Because of the disease that has no remedy, and that people come to you and bow to you and you feel that you deserve that respect" was the answer. Bayazid said, "Now, you have overcome me and I cannot defeat you anymore." When Bayazid was nearing his death, he wanted to know more about the secret of the above statement; and it was as is referred in the Koran: "Take Thou my soul (when I die) as one submitting to Thy Will, and unite me with the righteous" 12/101; and avoid that leads you to fear. The self-centered soul can be cured by means of oppression and force. However, it can be organized through knowledge and patience. Well! This is enough. If you want to see what I have said, go and see Rumi (Mak.M.II 49).

Bayazid and a Sheikh:

Bayazid was in the habit of going to Haj many times. When he traveled, on the way he would visit the Sheikhs of the city. Once when he arrived at Basra, a Sheikh asked him, "Bayazid, where are bound to?" His answer was, "I am going to Mecca, where God's house is." Upon this the Sheikh asked, "How much money have you got on you?"

Bayazid said he had two hundred dinars with him. The Sheikh said, "Alright, get up and turn seven times around me and give the silver coins to me." Bayazid gave the money to him and kissed his hands. "Where you are bound to is God's house and my heart is also His house. Ever since they have built that house, He has not visited it; but ever since my heart has become His abode, He has never vacated it" said the Sheikh (Per. 320/Tur.124).

Ahmed Ghazali:

Ahmed Ghazali wasn't a famous man (like his brother Imam-i Ghazali) because he had a difficult job, which kept his personality concealed behind a curtain and that curtain was not raised to anyone. He was great on his own. When he was trying to raise his curtain (to see the spiritual world), he heard a voice or was inspired, "Sheikh of Zengan will undo the curtain of your eyes". Upon this the master stood up and the same day he found the Sheikh. He found the Sheikh performing sema, and there he found what he was looking for. From there he went to Tabriz. People of Tabriz said, "This man has come to see that handsome young man. They gave money to an old woman and told her to stay on Ahmed's way. When he reached that old woman, he asked her, "What happened to you that you are moaning like this?" The woman replied, "Why shouldn't I cry, I have lost my son, who was an apple of my eyes and my flesh and blood". Ahmed asked, "Has he died?" The woman said, "Very much so". Ahmed asked the permission of his fellow travelers for one hour to find out whether the woman was right. All agreed and they gave a break. Ahmed was rapt meditating until dawn. When he came to himself he said, "This woman is telling a lie, I have visited almost all the souls created since Adam, and I have not found that young man's soul among them". Then they began their journey to Tabriz, when they arrived there a warm welcome was waiting for Ahmed. It may not be reasonable to disclose here that Ahmed had interest in beautiful faces. It was not because of lust but because he was able to see what others couldn't see. He had no sexual desires even if he would be forced to involve. Some liked his behavior while some did not (Tur.313-314).

Note: Sheikh Ahmed Ghazali (died in 1123 at Gazna) was a disciple of Abubekir Nijasi and Imam-i Ghazali's brother. His full name was Majd al-Din abu Fetih Ahmed bn. Muhammad Ghazali al- Tusi. He taught at Baghdad as a Muslim scholar. He has many treatises on religious law (Fiqh) and philosophy. One of his works "Sawanih fi al-Ishq" (Events of Love) seems to have good infuence on Shams and Rumi. However, he gives more importance to love God than *Shariah* unlike his brother. Here are some of his words about love: "A beloved is in every respect a beloved; and therefore, is without any demand while a lover is full of demand for his Beloved (for other details see Molla Jami's Nafahat ul-Uns).

Ahmed Ghazali and his two brothers belonged to a noble family. All of them were unique in their fields of studies. Specially, Muhammad Ghazali was perfect in many branches of knowledge. His works were brighter than the sun. Rumi knows it. Ahmed Ghazali had become unique sultan (a great master) in Gnosticism and Divine Knowledge. Even a deaf theologian would be bewildered by his speech. How can an ordinary man explain my words? I swear, if Rumi wanted to do it, he would do it better than me; and would decorate them with rich metaphors and deep meanings. Despite of all this, he may not be able to say exactly what I mean. Now, let me tell you about the third brother Omar Ghazali. He was a big business man and in generosity no one was his equal. Somebody said to Muhammad Ghazali "There is a rumor that your brother Ahmed delivers speeches but he has no knowledge." Upon this Muammad Ghazali sent his book entitled 'Zahire' and he warned the carrier: "Go and sit beside my brother with respect and keep an eye on his each gesture. Don't miss his smiles, movements of his head and hands, and when your eyes meet his eyes be extra careful. Watch him from top to toe." When the messenger reached the Tekke, he saw Ahmed Ghazali sitting there in good mood. As soon as they came face to face, the master asked, "Have you brought us a book?" These words shook the messenger's body. Then the master spoke, "I am *Ummi* (illiterate), yet it is different from *Ami* (blind). Ami means total blind in knowledge, but Ummi means a person who cannot read and write." Then he requested the messenger to read the book. The frightened messenger began to read the book from here and there. Then the master said, "Now write these lines at the beginning of the book:

I don't need 'Zahire', what have I to do with the book?
When I have my Beloved's lips, I don't care for wine!
(Tur.309).

Note: Imam-i Ghazali (Ebu Hamid ibn Muhammad ibn Muhammad Ghazali) was born in Tus (a town of Khorasan) in A.D.1058. He had deep knowledge in theology and philosophy. He tried to create a balance between Shariah (Muslim Law) and Tassavuf (Islamic Mysticism). He has about 120 works and is called 'Hujet ul-Islam' (The column of Islam). (for other details see Cavit Sunar, İslam Tassuvufu Tarihi, Ankara University 143, p.52-56 and Hilmi Ziya Ülken, İslam Düşüncesi, Istanbul University p. 284- 297).

About Omar Khayyam:

"No one ever reached the secret of love
Those who did were confounded."

Sheikh Ibrahim (a disciple of Shams) objected to the above lines of Omar Khayyam saying, "Why should one who reaches the secret of love become confounded?" I replied, "He is telling his own situation. He was confounded. Sometimes he blames the heaven or fate or God. There are times when he denies his belief, and then proves just the opposite. Some other time when he says something, he says out of deep suspicion. A (true) believer of God never confounds, because God opens His veil to him. He knows exactly what to ask for and is ready for submission openly. His great pleasure is to see God openly from the west to the east.

An infidel always thinks negatively and uses first personal pronoun 'I'. He has no doubt in his I-ness, because he can see his own (physical) activities openly. Why should he doubt about common things as eating, tasting etc. He does not have to accept anything else said by others. It is like this situation: Suppose someone comes towards you at the daybreak, a stick in his hand and walking by resting on a wall with the other hand. He is trembling, crying and moaning. Then he shouts and says, "What is the matter? The sun hasn't risen yet (it is dark everywhere). Another person joins him the event and says, "I feel the same way. I am worried the sun hasn't risen yet. Why the day has been late?" You see the day has already dawned, and there is full light everywhere. If thousands of people say like the blind man, one will only laugh at them. So is the case with the believer. He sees light openly, but the problem is that there aren't many believers of that character (Per. 354-355/ Tur II. 154).

Muhammad Ghazali and Omar Khayyam:

Muhammad Ghazali once read Ibn. Sina's work "Al Isharat Wetenbihhat" to Omar Khayyam. Ibn Sina (Avicenna) was a highly learned man. Some claim that Ghazali has made use of Avicenn's Isharat in his great work 'Ihya-i Ulumiddin'. Ghazali read the book twice but Khayyam failed to understand it. When he read the third time, he (Ghazali) ordered the musicians and the drum players to come out and play the music so that Sina's book may become popular:

If anyone who just claims the stage of 'Analhaq'
Deserves to be hanged by the same rope (like Mansur).
(Per. 207-208 /Tur. II. 16).

Note: Ibn Sina, known as Avicenna in Europe was born in a town near Bukhara and lived between the years 980-1037. He is considered to be one of the most learned person in the Islamic history. He learnt the Holy Koran by heart when he was only ten years old. He accomplished his studies of Islamic law, astronomy, medicine, physics, logic and philosophy at the age of eighteen and he wrote many books on the above subjects. He studied Akhwan ul-Safa carefully and deepened his knowledge about Platonism, Aristotelianism, Neo-Platonism, Galenism and Farabianism etc. that he brought within the frame of Islam.

Rabiya Adaviya:

Rabiya once said, "I sent my heart to the world to observe it. After that I sent it to the spiritual world so that it may see that world too; it never came back" (Per.p.200).

Note: Rabiya Adaviya (died in A.D.801) was a great woman sufi, who discovered divine love and held above everything as she says, "My God if I pray to Thee for fear of Hell, put me in Hell; and if I pray to Thee so that I may go to Paradise, then close the gate of Paradise on me. If I pray to Thee only for Thy love, then do not deprive me of

Thy beautiful and eternal vision (Jamal). (for full detail see 'First Among Sufis', Widad al-Skaini, Trans. by Dr.Nabil Safwat, The Octagon Press, London.

Hakim Senai:

Senai murmured some lines when he was dying. Somebody gave ears to his lips and heard this:

I give up all, all what I have uttered and said,

Because there is no meaning left in words and words in meaning (Per.233).

Note: Senai and Attar (great Persian poets) were Rumi's favorites like his father and his first master Burahneddin. Actually, the Masnevi carries their tone as Eflaki (6/3) narrates: One day Husammedin requested Rumi, "Sir, if you wrote a book like Sheikh Hakim Senai's "Ilahinama" in the meter of Feriddudin Attar's "Mantik Uttayir" it will remain for ever among the coming generation. Senai's full name was Abu al-Majd Majdud Senai (died in A.D. 1140) and he, generally, wrote about the disappointment of love towards God, while Rumi changed this concept into a more positive view.

Shahab al-Din Suhrawardi (Maqtul):

People went to Shahab and listened to his many wise and interesting lectures and they made use of them by bowing (agreeing) to what the philosopher said. When the listeners came out, they would say, "He is a philosopher and as a philosopher he knows everything". I deleted his name from my list on the ground that he was no God to know everything. Then I wrote these words "Yes he is a philosopher so he must know everything" But you know he denied the doomsday saying, "When the universe stop rotating the doomsday will come". "How can the universe stop its rotation if no universe is left?" I asked myself. Some claim that the prophets were wise men and they said things like these for people (to understand). Khalif Ali once said, "If every matter is as easy as you say, then we are all free (to think the way we want)". Nevertheless, in such (spiritual) matters human beings are helpless. So let us wrap up this issue. This matter is mentioned like this in the Koran: 'On the day when the earth will be transformed into a different earth, including the heavens will come forth to God, the One, the Almighty' 14/48. 'And that day We shall roll up the heavens as a recorder rolls up a written scroll exactly the way We began the creation before..21/104'. Now, think! When God changes this physical universe and the earth into something else, so what are the philosophers after? These discussions are worthless (Per. 221 / Tur. II. 29).

Shahabeddin sometime would speak blasphemy, but he had a clean heart and spiritual height. His soul had dominated his body, and he ate very little. One day, I was speaking about symbols and explained the meaning of them. I wanted to explain them to Shahabeddin as well. I said, "You hold that the universe does not dependent on its parts but on its wholeness. Why are you so concerned with the wholeness (totality)? I also speak about totality, and I believe that the parts are not separate from its wholeness. Certainly, if you claim for the parts only then how is the totality possible? If a garden has no trees in it, it is not a garden; it can only be a rock". Shahab replied, "Well, I don't say this to hurt someone that the totality does not depend on its parts. Suppose I have an insect settled in my stomach, sleeping there temporarily and I am not aware of it, what harm it makes if I know it or not?" (Per. 285 / Tur. II.90).

Shahabeddin, whom they also called *Maqtul* (the assassinated), was loved and respected by the Emir of Aleppo (Zahir) and, because of this people were jealous of him. Now, some planned to kill him. They all requested the King (Selaheddin Ayubi) to issue an order to the authorities to put Shahab in a catapult and hurl him. When the authorities received the letter, they pulled down Shahab's turban and had his head cut off (by mistake). When the Emir Zahir (son of Sultan Selaheddin Eyubi) understood the trick, he ordered the assassins to lick Shahab's blood like dogs. Two other were executed for planning the trick, and some were sold as slaves for good price for forty Dinars as special gifts. A good manuscript of a small copy of the Koran was sold for five Dirhem (silver cents) only, because a few understood it.

Shahab had a desire to ban silver and gold coins (the money) and to use something else instead, because they were the source of crimes and murders and this may be disobedience to Islam. If people ask me, "Was he not strict follower of the Muhammadan path (*Shariah*)?" My answer will be negative. One day Shahabeddin was discussing about military affairs. The king said, "What do you know about army?" Just then the king saw soldiers all around with naked swords, up the roofs and on the earth. The king rose up and went to his treasury (for safety) and conspired to have him killed without further enquiry (Per. 350 /Tur.II 150).

Shahab's knowledge was dominant over his intelligence; although it is best that intelligence should rule over knowledge. His brain, which is the center for knowledge, had weakened. To strengthen his brain, he would take one or two glasses of wine, but not more. Due to this weakness, he couldn't deal with Asad Muteklim's witty talks, who would swear him ultimately (ibid).

In Damascus, those dogs called Shahab 'an infidel' openly. Why should he be an infidel for he was spiritually enlightened? Yes, when compared to Shams he may be infidel, but if he could join his service, he might change into a full moon (Per.329).

Note: His full name was Sheikh ul-Ishraq Abu al- Fattah Shahabeddin Suhrawardi and was born in the Iranian side of Azerbaijan, and was assassinated in A.D.1191, soon after Shams had met him in Damascus. Like İkhawan ul-Safa, he tried to bring the Greek and Eastern philosophy in the scope of Islam. For this reason he was not welcomed in Damascus or elsewhere. He was founder of the illuminationism (Ishraqiya) school and followed the teaching of Neo-Platonism (see Hilmi Ziya). His two great works 'Hiqmat ul-Ishraq (the Wisdom of Illumination)' and 'Heyaqil al-Nur (The Statues of Light)' are famous. His method is based on irrational intuition. He held that one couldn't reach the reality by depending on only intelligence and observation. One has to live the reality by oneself to conceive it. When man gets rid of carnal desires, he also gets rid of imaginations and contacts the world of Divine Light (Nur ul-Ilah), where all the realities of creation are disclosed (also see Hossein Ziai, HIP, p.434).

Fahreddin-i Razi:

Fahreddin was a philosopher or at least he was one of them. When he met with Sultan Khuwarizmshah he said to him, "I have studied fundamentals of all branches of knowledge and I have made a comparative survey of all essential books written so far since Plato. They are all in my mind clearly, and with differences. I have also studied other books written before Plato and I know their scopes. I have severely criticized my contemporaries. Consequently, I have digested all of them". After this statement, he began to speak about all the fields of study he had accomplished and claimed that he had undone all doubts there were to be faced. He became Emir and friend of the Sultan. There spread a gossip among people and they would say, "You have another art in you, you are infidel". Thanks to God that you (Rumi) are free from that kind of scandal... I saw some people who were filled with fear and when I forwarded they said to me, "Be careful, a monster has appeared that will devour the entire world as a single morsel". I felt no fear and I proceeded until I came to an iron gate awfully huge on which a heavy lock hung. People told me that was the spot where the monster with seven heads abode, and they warned me. When I happened to be inside I saw nothing but a small worm, which I crushed under my feet and killed. Only God knows better!

As a matter of fact, all his words are like worms and so are his books. If someone knows the meaning of 'Elif' (the first letter of the word Allah) he does not need to know anything else for the rest comes automatically (Per. 221-222 /Tur.II 30).

Shahabeddin taught in Damascus and said, "To my logic God is not bound to His will, but to His delightment (of His tastes)". While Fahreddin-i Razi, having been richly fed and bestowed by gold and honors by the king, said, "God does what He desires". Shahabeddin said, "Well life for me is like a heavy burden on me: burden on my neck and my legs in the mud, helpless as an old man who needs help to be recued" (Per. 220 /Tur.II.29).

Note: Fahreddin-i Razi was an Islamic philosopher who wrote more than a hundred books on all cultural fields of Islam. He passed away in the year 1209, and is considered to be the second Ghazali of the 13th century. Shahabeddin and Razi were Majd al-Din Jili's students. Razi wrote about many subjects such as logic, mathematics, metaphysics, astronomy, medicine, esoteric sciences, criticism on the Greek philosophy, Koranic commentaries etc. However, he was not deep in the Divine Knowledge (Ilm-e Ledun) and love of God gained via contemplation and yearning, which comes only from God and one must not be proud of that because it does not belong to human being. This is why Rumi's father, Shams and Rumi himself didn't like him (for further information on Razi see Hosein Nasr, HIP, p.642 and M,Saghir's preface to 'Ilmul Akhlaq', Kitab Bhawan, New Delhi).

Juneyd al-Baghdadi:

Once, children pointed at Juneyd saying that he was the man who spent all nights for God. Juneyd thought, "It is not good to disappoint the kids". So he gave up sleeping at nights and sat praying until daybreaks. Now, may the blessings of the believers go to him (Bayazid)! There are saints who try to hide themselves, while God wants to expose Himself in many ways. Wakefulness was the part of Juneyd's life but when he went weak, people suggested him to sleep over nights (Per. 321/ Tur.II. 125).

The story of Juneyd and Ahmed-i Zindiq:

This is the story: People suggested Juneyd to meet with Ahmed-i *Zindiq* (the infidel) because he was the only one to solve his spiritual problems, and if he did not go, he would never be able to achieve the divine knowledge even if he offered prayers all his life. So he set out from Baghdad to the town where he was to find the Zindiq. Now he realized that it would not be decent to call him Zindiq (atheist or infidel). Thus he changed his name into Ahmed-i *Saddiq* (Ahmed the faithful) and began to ask people, "Where does Ahmed the Faithful live?" He went around the town asking for the address, but all in vain. He searched for the man for sixty days without any result. Finally, when he was passing by a ruined mosque, he heard someone reciting the Koran from the part on Joseph. His heart moved. Then he saw a young man coming out of the mosque. This time Juneyd decided to ask for the man with his real name, and he asked the young man. The young man said, "Haven't you heard the recitation?" Upon this answer, Juneyd fell down due to extreme excitement and the young man gave him a hand. Juneyd had found the man by telling the truth.

Note: It is better to avoid (*Tavil,* usage of words by allusions in spiritual affairs.

Abu al-Qasim bn Muhammad al-Junayd al- Baghdadi (d. A.D.910) was a great Imam of his time. For *Tasssawuf* (Islamic Mysticism) he said, "It means that God causes you to die to yourself so that He may give you rebirth in Him" and "Selfness is so bad that it puts the owner into dangers and leads him to total disaster" and "The state of annihilation means to attain perfection, in other words to achieve transfiguration to be eternal with God".

Uways al-Qirani:

Uways al-Qirani could not see the Prophet Muhammad (PUH) physically when he was still alive. He was not empty, curtains were raised on him and the sickness of her mother had kept him at home by the will of God. The Prophet had informed his friends and the Caliph Omar about his existence saying, "If he comes after my death, give him my regards and don't talk to him in details. After the Prophet's death, his mother passed away. He visited Muhammad's grave in the absence of the great Caliphs. Other friends of Muhammad asked him questions and he told them about his excuse and his situation. They asked him, "When it comes to serving the Prophet, there can be no excuse of mother or father. Our comrades and we have killed the infidel like flies and mosquitoes for sake of love of the Prophet. There is no place for any personal feelings or obligations." They were holding him guilty despite of his explanations, and their talk prolonged. Turning his face to them he asked, "How long have you been in the service of the Prophet?" They told him the duration of their attachments and added that each day was like thousands of years and they couldn't say more:

If for a moment you perchance to meet with your friend in privacy,
That is the time when you get all that chance can provide you,
So be aware, and do not loose the opportunity of being with your friend,
For you may not get such a great chance again in your life.

Uways asked the group, "Alright, what was the sign of Prophet Muhammad?" Some tried to tell about

Prophet's height and form, while others told him about his wisdom and knowledge ability and how he spent nights for prayers. Uways said again, "I am not asking for that kind of signs. If the caliphs were there, they would not ask about his identity because they would recognize him as is said, "Seeing is not like hearing":

See my face like the gold of time and don't ask,
See my tears like the grains of the pomegranate and don't ask,
Don't ask me about the state of the inside of my house,
See the blood at the threshold of the house and don't ask.

The friends of the Prophet failed to answer his questions and told him that they had no knowledge about any other answer and they pleaded; "Now you tell us". As soon as he opened his mouth to say something, many fainted away and fell down and while some began to cry in ecstasy. Uways said no more, and people had no courage to ask further (Per. 332/Tur.133-134).

Note: Uways Qarani was a Yemenite cotemporary o Muhammad, who failed to meet with him despite of his great will. He was later killed in a war against the enemy. His followers believe in direct contact with God.

Hallaj al-Mansur:

A full exposure of the spiritual light was not yet given to Hallaj, if he were, he would never say, "*Anal Haq* = I am God" because the Reality is far from I-ness. What is

I-ness? What are these Arabic letters 'Elif' and 'Nun'? If he had totally submerged in the spiritual world, all the letters would have no space including 'Elif' or 'Nun' in that world. Someone said, "God is One". I said to him, "What difference it makes to you because you are still in this divisible world composed of thousands of atoms (particles); and each particle in this world is separated, withered and congealed that is He Himself. His Being is *Qadim* (without begging or end). It does not concern you since you are non-existent and helpless and weak in the Presence of Divine light.

Muhammad once said, "Poverty is my pride" although he was not capacitated in the entire universe but he was proud of his poverty and humbleness. He was helpless and weak in the Presence of Divine Light. His chest burnt because of that light yet he said, "I wish I had thousands of chests like these to burn away, fall a part and perish" (Per. 334 /Tur.II.137).

Note: 'Elif' the first Arabic letter means Allah (God) and His Oneness and the letter 'Nun' means the light of God or Divine Enlightenment.

Muhi al-Din Arabi and Shams:

During his conversation Sheikh Muhammad (Ibn ul-Arabi) repeated this sentence: "He was mistaken and that was a mistake". I noticed that he made mistakes himself, and when he did so, I would correct him, which made him lower his head. Then he would say, "My son you are slashing the mountain" although I had no such purpose.

However, most of the time such conversations lead to further discussions and he surrendered to me suggestions. For example, he experienced a state and he would talk about that. I would show him how he stayed at that stage. One day, we came to the discussion that any words of Muhammad (*Hadis*) that suited the Koran were the correct ones. He quoted one Hadis and asked, "Where is its relative verse in the Koran?" Meantime, I noticed that he was in a strange state. I did not want him to leave that individual sate and come back to the collective one. I kept answering in accordance with his questions. Once I said, "The Hadis you have quoted carries doubt whether it belongs to Muhammad or not? And where is the reference in the Koran to this Hadis? 'The learned are like one soul'. Thinking that I was asking him a question, he replied quickly, "All believers (Mulims) are brothers" 40/10 and " Your creation and your rising (from the dead) are only as a single soul" 31/28. When he felt that I did not mean to ask him a question, and realized my purpose (which was just to inform), he said again, "Son! You lash me severely" and began to smile because the word 'Son' didn't suit the situation (Per. 298 / Tur. 102).

From time to time Sheikh Muhammad would prostrate and would bow his head in prayers and would say, "I am follower of *Shariah* (Islamic law) but he was not very submissive to it. I benefited a lot from his knowledge, although not as much as from you (Rumi). Your children do not understand you. Strange, perhaps they do not understand themselves. However, you have no obligation to expose yourself spiritually to them or others (Per.357 /Tur. II.156).

Note: Muhyi al-Din Muhammad ibn Ali ibn al-Arabi (shortly known as Ibn al- Arabi) lived during the years A.D. 1165-1240. He was the most outstanding personality in the history of Islamic mysticism. His lovers call him "Sheikh ul-Akbar = the great Sheikh". His pantheistic views made him famous in India, Iran, Turkey and the central Asia. He seems to be under Suharawardi's doctrine of Light and darkness. Among his more than five hundred books two 'Futuhat al-Makkiyya (Opennings of Mecca)' and Fusus al-Hikam. He claimed that he got all the knowledge through divine inspiration and Muhammad's soul. He held that only God's existence is the Reality the rest is only God's emanation and procession (*Zuhur*). He was born at Murcia (Spain) and belonged to a noble family. He was once a secretary to the government in Spain. He traveled extensively in Islamic lands and visited Anatolia. In Konya he married Sheikh Sadreddin's widowed mother. Sadreddin studied pantheistic views under his custody but later gave up his views. Shams had a chance to see him in Damascus, where the master lived between the years 1223-1240 (for other full details see W.C.Chittick, *The Sufi Path of Knowledge,* and *The Self Disclosure of God,* State University, New York Press, Introduction.)

Ahwaddudin-i Kirmani:

There are God's secret lovers whom God covers up and tells them His secrets. Once the Sheikh Awhaddudin-i Kirmani invited me to *Sema* (transcendental dance) and showed me great respect. Then he took me to his privacy and requested me to stay with him. I said, "I will stay with you under one condition- Sit and drink wine with me in front of your disciples while I wouldn't drink". He said, "Why won't you drink?" I replied, "So that you become a lucky sinner and I become an unlucky sinner". After this, he uttered no words and struck his hands against his head (Per. 347-348 / Tur.II.148).

Note: Awhaddudin-i Kirmani (A.D.1166-1238) was a disciple of Ruknuddin Sujjasi, whom Shams had met in Baghdad. Kirmani's full name was Ewhaddudin Hamid bn Ebi'l – Fahr el-Kirmani. He was a great Sufi and a poet of Anatolia and friend of the Great Sheikh Ibn ul-Arabi. He also traveled all over central Asia and the Arab lands. He believed in God's vision in human beings and in handsome young persons (Wahdet-i Shuhud = Unity of Divine Manifestation).

Asad Mutekellim:

One day Asad Mutekellim (a theologian of Sivas, Turkey) was explaining the meaning of this Koranic verse: "Wherever you are, God is with you". Despite of being a good scholar he would go mad if someone asked him questions in front of people. I asked him, "You say God is with us, how is it possible?" He replied, "You are only a little kid, what do you have to do with this question". Although he had tendency to kindness, yet he would be angry and say what he wanted to say. I insisted, "Tell me how it is possible?" He swore me and said that I had formed the habit of asking questions. Then he replied, "God is with us by means of knowledge". I said, "But knowledge is not separate from God's Being, neither is any of His attributes". He said, "These are the old questions (asked many times before)". I said again, "But the new are born of the old". You see, what kind of a *Mutekellim* (a religious orator) he was?

Sultan Bahaeddin Veled (Rumi's father):

Bahaeddin had seen in dream that he had fallen in black water and shouted for help to me requesting me to hold his hand. I did not do that, so he floated away. Bahaeddin thought if I had mentioned him about the dream, and commented over that the dream would have been true. But if I made no mention of the dream, it will be the production of his mind. I felt it, but I did not tell him (Per. 203 /Tur. II/2).

Note: This is the proof that Shams had good relation with Rumi's father (to learn more about his father please see The Essence of Rumi p.13-16).

Alaeddin Chelebi:

I wish to expose some matters to you by means of symbols and allusions; although it may sound awkward. I am confident that you will excuse me for this impertinence. Let me explain: Water has a single source, but sometime it flows in different branches. One branch draws the water to one side, and the other to another side.

Nevertheless, if someone reaches the source and submerges in it, he frees himself from the separate branches. Similarly, if you choose a branch of a tree, you may fall down with it. When you choose the whole tree (its trunk etc.) you are strong even if one branch gives way, you have other to hold on. In the street of the Beloved there is *Bhang* (Canabis Sativa), and when you take it, it makes you mad, and you cannot find your way to the house of your Beloved. How can such a mad man be considered wise? Not all have this wisdom of understanding (Per. 204 / Tur.II. 12).

Note: The above statement is a proof that Rumi's younger son Alaeddin Chelebi did not follow Shams' and Rumi's way of love. He had tendency to more fanatic way of Islam. Ultimately, he was against Shams in the end, while Rumi's elder son Sultan Veled founded *Mevleviye* (Rumi's sect) and put it into a system.

On Sema (the Transcendental Dance):

During a Sema illumination and divine vision is strong in the God-loving men. They step out of their physical body and by passing through certain stages they reach God. However, there is another kind of Sema, the performance of which is sin. The Sema performed by lovers of God is legal, and to think it illegal is a sin. Of course those hands that do not rise up for sake of God will burn in Hell and those that are raised up for love of God deserve paradise. This kind of Sema is as obligatory as five time prayers or fasting. When such lovers perform

Sema, they are aware of each other in all parts of the world (Per.19 /Tur.38)

Sema is right for those God-loving people because they do everything for God, when they hate or love they are sincere. If they swear a staunch infidel, he becomes a believer. He changes into a saint and goes to paradise (Per.22/ Tur.43).

What is the use of a physical Sema? It is like eating and feeding the body which improves sensual feelings as is said, "The infidel eat and drink like cattle" 47/ 12

We hear that there are Semas being performed and congregations held in Konya. We haven't seen any. In other words they don't offer any spiritual states or interesting speeches (Tur.254).

During Sema a man wears special dresses which others don't wear normally (Per. 175 / Tur. 351).

Note: This means that even at the time of Shams, Sema-dress was special and was not invented after Rumi's death.

There was Sema being performed with nice music and melodious voice, but it did not appeal to the clean-hearted Sufis. The Sheikh said, "Have a look at he shoes outside to see if there is a stranger, because intellect leads only to the door but it does not show into the inner part of the house, where intellect, heart and everything is a curtain. We have friends in Churches and in Temples" (Per. 246 / Tur. II. 52).

Once during Sema a disciple of Sheikh Shahbeddin recited a verse. Upon this the Sheikh (who was mastering the Sema) said, "May your neck be broken and your tongue be sheared. Who could dare recite a verse in a place, where God has disclosed Himself and has raised His curtains and has become all eyes? It is not decent to talk at that place. He who has not reached at that stage deserves to be insulted like the filth in a house or a black ugly naked man filled with sensual desires among handsome people. Just then, I noticed that my chest was filled with light like that of the sun and it came out of me as a candle light. I turned my face quickly and my turban fell down. The Sheikh held up his turban and said, "I am seeing in myself, my veins, bones and blood and all my soul; and when I see them, I see nothing else (Per 208).

Note: In real Sema you may see strange things like above.

Somebody said to me, "You have blemished the name of good learned people with Sema." I replied, "Don't you know only those who practice Sema can differentiate between a believer and non-believer, and what is good and what is bad." He said again, "Can you go to God by dancing?" I replied, "Well, you can dance, too, and go to God by taking only two steps" (Per. 276 /Tur.II.82).

Other General Topics:

People and Shams' Advice:

Let me tell you something, these people (common folk) like hypocrisy and they hate truth. For instance, I said to a man, "You are a great man and a unique personality of this age". He was over delighted, and holding my hand he said, "I missed you very much. This is my fault (that I ignored you)" Last year I told him the truth (about him), he became my enemy. This is not so strange; you have to live with these people hypocritically to pass nice time (Per. 61 / Tur. 99).

Don't bear the company of those who are plunged in worldly desires, pump and show because they will darken your soul. Take care of yourself so that your personality does not give way to negative changes. Your religious garments, that you wear, do not provide regular insight. I always sat and stood modestly, and I felt little interest in showy people (Per.99 /Tur.154).

There is a *Hadis*, "Monastic life is forbidden" which does not mean that one should always mix up with people or watch them from a distance, but talk to them about the truth plainly. And after some time, if someone comes to you and says that the secret of your speech (that you delivered) is different, and explains it otherwise, and gives the (spiritual) meaning that is far from the sound and letters of the words, then be submissive to him. When he explains further secrets of the talk and shows you their proofs, leaving other simple details for ordinary people, and you notice awe and greatness of God in his face, he is our younger brother (our man). But such a man must also have some feelings of pain and yearnings because they burn away the hesitance (skepticism) and doubts (Per. 102 /Tur. 159).

A man said, " My God! After I end up with my struggles will You expose on me the other world that you say is behind this mirror (physical world) from thence I see Your light. Now, I have lost my energy so give me more. The answer was, "Yes, but you have to move on further if you want it". The man said, "My Lord! I am trying to move on but it is difficult for me to move any further". Like a barber who first gives some nuts and dry grapes to a child to soothe before using the razor, God makes a man busy with the worries first and then bestows upon him His light. Previously, the mirror of the man was broken and he, who first possessed love of God, now begins to possess God Himself (Per. 148 / Tur. 221).

On drugs and wine:

"Our friends enjoy intoxication with hashish," said someone. I said, "This is a diabolic idea. Even angels' fantasy is not permissible here (in our company). Why shouldn't our friends enjoy our infinite universe, which makes a man so drunk that he looses his senses? This kind of drunkenness is acceptable but wine is forbidden". Somebody said, "Wine is prohibited in the Koran while hashish is not". I answered, "All the verses of the Koran are based on a reason, and for that reason they are revealed. Hashish wasn't taken at the time of Prophet Muhammad. If any friends of Muhammad happened to use it, he would have issued orders to execute him (Per. 21 / Tur. 40).

I had told them not to drink wine in my presence. One of them said, "We are expert in theology, we have our own mosque and medrise, and we don't have to worry". I was not intimated by that kind of speech. My dress won't get wet even if I am put in a pitcher of wine. I can offer my ritual prayers as usual and this cannot give me any harm. However, this is my habit that I am afraid of a drunkard since my childhood and I fear that he might fall right on me (Tur. 258).

Forgetfulness is of three kinds:

The first forgetfulness is to forget the other world for this world. The second is to forget this world for the other one. Some work for the other world and neglect this world and forget even their own presence. For them this world is like a mouse in the hand of a cat (they can play with it). They gain the spiritual uplift, by listening to the sermons of a saint, which a Sheikh cannot obtain by dint of prayers in thirty years. The third kind of forgetfulness is to forget this as well as the other world for love of God (Per.23 /Tur.44).

Microcosm and Macrocosm:

The learned think that microcosm is concealed in the creation of man and the macrocosm is the outer space that surrounds us. For prophets it is just the opposite: the outer universe is microcosm and the macrocosm is hidden in them (Tur. 227).

The act of seeing God differs from person to person:

A disciple said, "I see God seventy times (many times) a day. His sheikh said, "Your seeing Bayazid is many times better than seeing God. When the disciple came out of the oak forest he happened to see Bayazid and died instantly because he was a lover, and he died in the way of seeking a beloved. In other words, a very small portion of his ego was left and it came to an end. But a poor sighted disciple sees only his own image and cannot see God through the eyes of Bayazid. Similarly, Bayazid cannot see God like Moses (Tur. 277).

On Fear of Death:

As once Muhammad (P.U.H) said, " Believers never die, but they only transfer". Thus, death is different from transfer. Man cannot find comfort and pleasure in a dark narrow house or even stretch his legs. But when he passes from that house to a larger one or to a palace with large gardens and running waters, he cannot be dead. This should be clear enough. If you have enough light and desire to die (without fear), then may God bless you! And do not forget me in your prayers. In case you have no such thing then try to obtain it, and struggle for it as the Koran tells us: "Then express your desire for death, if you are truthful" (62/ 6 a message to the Jews). There are true lovers among the believers, men and women, who seek death (are not afraid of death). (Per.28 / Tur.51).

Satan can appear in any shape:

Prophet Muhammad once desired to see the real face of Satan; and he noticed that on all his faces God was manifest. So how could now any desire to see Satan's face be left? To save you from headache let me tell you: "If Satan wants to put on a spiritual form, he puts it on in such a way that you may even dislike God. However, if you give up the desire of seeing him (Satan), he never bothers you again. Well don't trust yourself too much in this matter, because Satan can show up from any door at any time to deceive you (Tur.224).

An Advice:

O you rash fellow! If you can't say a word about my outer state, how can you tell anything about my inner state? O my Lord! My Merciful God! Any belief that pleases you and warms you hold that tight; and any belief that is cold for you, leave aside. A real good man is a person who can manage to be happy in face of unhappiness, and in sadness he knows how to be pleased. He knows well that wishes come true after disappointments. Who can tell? May be your disappointment is intertwined with success. Sometime there is a hope in disappointment and there is a fear of disappointment hidden in success. That day, I had a fit of fever and I was happy that I should recover the next day. When I was healthy, I had the fear of falling sick again. If you say that the food you hadn't eaten that day, you wouldn't have pains in your stomach, and then you are only bothering about that in vain (for that has gone now). A good man is a person who handles everything on his own and he is great for that nature (Per.194 / Tur. 374).

Be forgiving:

If you can look at your enemy with love, do it because if you go to someone's door with love, it can change hatred into love. Your enemy expects hatred and anger from you, but if you take love to him, he will like it (Per. 35 /Tur. 61).

Are Sultans Shadow of God?

It is said that Sultans are shadows of God on earth. The divine world is light upon light, taste after taste, glory upon glory and mercy upon mercy. The shadow (of Sultan) we see is nothing but show of this world, filth, ugliness, tastelessness and mortality. Then how can they be shadow of God? Nevertheless, if there is a Sultan with fine character, he is praise worthy. A tree has its value for its fruits and if it has no fruit, it deserves fire (Per.142 / Tur.215).

Sign of the good and the bad:

Let me tell you the sign of those who deserve paradise and of those who deserve hell. Ever since God has created this universe, like an arrow darted out of its bow, the gate of His Mercy opens and becomes wider every moment. The further explanation of this discussion will damage our minds. A man who shows broad mindedness and nature, and vast courage in speaking openly, and prays for the betterment of the entire world without discrimination; and you feel consolation at heart by speaking to him and forget your worries, is the man of paradise. In edition to his above qualities, you feel inner delight even if he swears you, and when you speak about God's unity you begin to cry and yet feel an inner satisfaction like Sheikh Serajeddin (a Sufi from Konya) in his presence. Now there is another kind of man who sucks people's blood, his speech is boring and unfriendly, and you feel no warmth towards him and his speech, is like Satan and deserves Hell (Per.146 / Tur.219).

On the creation of this world:

Far beyond this land of water and clay, behind the mountains of this visible world when we were mixed up like Gog and Magog there came a voice, "Get down". Thence we came down to this mean world. From a distance appeared a creature in totally dark and the non-existent world. There were no cities and trees in view from that distance. We were alien to this world. As we came closer and closer, the mischievous grains and traps began to appear. There would have been no world in existence, if we hadn't the pleasure of meeting the grain, which was more charming than the traps. It is said that Adam with tremendous surprise saw a stone that came towards him. He fell in love with that stone and ran fast to embrace it.

Note: For Gog and Magog see the Koran 18/95 and 21/96. They were wild worriers living in Central Asia whom Alexander the Great had to stop (for detail see Yusuf Ali's commentary p.760; The Holly Koran, Dar al-Arabia, Lebanon.).

Two attributes of man:

Man has two attributes 1- Supplication (pleading and asking) and 2- Contentment. What can be expected from these two attributes? What can be the ultimate desire of a seeker (needy)? Of course the beloved sought. Sheikh Muhammad (Shams' friend) said to an infidel, "Prostrate to the right direction (to Ka'ba) and say the right things." The infidel said, "My direction of prostration is you, but if I tell you who you really are you will deny me. In that case, you will become infidel and I a Muslim (a believer)". A Muslim looked for an infidel, but where is the infidel? If I find one I will prostrate to him, kiss him many times. Now you tell me the truth whether you are an infidel or not so that I also kiss you (Tur.299). Every atheist needs a Muslim and every Muslim needs an atheist. What pleasure do you have in being a Muslim? The pleasure is in being an atheist because you may not find true Islam in a Muslim, but an atheist may find the true Islamic way ultimately. You can say this is the hand of an atheist and kiss it, you think you have kissed atheism; and then you kiss a Muslim's hand and think that you have kissed Islam. As a matter of fact, in whichever hand is the Reality that hand should be kissed (Tur 301.).

Note: In Sufism 'hand' stands for the attribute of Divine Power. Islam (surrendering to God) is nobody's property. Any one can find the Truth and be a Muslim.

Creed is above patriotism:

Someone says that son of that man has become disciple of a person from Tabriz (Shams). How can a Khorasanian be obedient to a Tabrazi? Now, that man claims to be a Sufi and a pious man. Can he be so stupid as to believe in regional patriotism? If an Istanbulian claims that Mecca belongs to this world and the creed does not belong to this world, then the Meccanian has to accept the idea of Istanbulian. The meaning of this Hadis, "Patriotism is the part of belief" does not mean Mecca, which is a part of this world while belief does not belong to this world as is said, "Islam came to this world as a stranger and went as a stranger" (Hadis of Muhammad). As Islam is alien to this world, and belongs to the other world then how can it depend on Mecca only? Those who believe in this way, they are still at the primary stage of love. However, to get rid of such believes is difficult (for common people). The first stage (of divine love) is intoxication and to avoid it is extremely cumbersome. In order to pass by this stage one has to be fast and active. Next is the wantonness imposed by the spiritual world. One hasn't seen the soul yet, but its intoxication is severe. Due to this intoxication, one regards no prophets and saints and avoids reciting of Hadis and the verses of the Koran. He feels embarrassed to quote words from any other sources and to disclose them to public. To pass by the second stage is also difficult unless a man of God comes and reveals on him the reality of the soul. At the third stage intoxication continues strongly but it is closer to soberness because whatever one thinks as God, God takes it from him. At the third stage God intoxicates one, which is perfection. At this stage one has full soberness and universal intellect.

As for divine love we don't want to discuss about love of women and riches of this world; and not to go around the world for fear of loosing intoxication. There are many monks who expose such feelings from time to time. Imad (Imaduddin bn Shahabuddin Suhrawardi) had perfect intoxication of divine love and had spiritual scent by which he found his way to God. Awhad (Awhaduddin Kirmani) was close to perfection of love intoxication. The sorcerers of Pharaoh were perfect in that too and scent of soul had reached them, but Pharaoh was incomplete and depended on his logic and, therefore, was wrong. The sorcerers had an art, which Pharaoh did not have. Seyyid Burhaneddin (Rumi's first teacher) had all perfection of love and intoxication. Rumi and he had the knowledge, which no other had. I discovered by knowledge that my Sheikh (Abu Bekir) had intoxication of love but he did not have the soberness that comes after that stage (Per. 133 /Tur. 203).

On Faith:

Any one who comes to this world brings something with him. Some bring show and strong worldly desires while some bring love. It is believed that love is eternal and immortal, but there are different opinions about soul. Some (philosophers) think it is eternal (*Qadim*), while others think that it is temporal i.e. it was created later (*Hadis*). But all the souls were created long time ago. As Prophet Muhammad said, "Souls are one group like soldiers". However, these groups are of different kinds. There are groups of tavern lovers and mischievous souls. But I shall talk about only that group which has pure souls. God is aware of all groups especially of the pious souls, as is said in the Koran says, "God is helper of those who perform their duties..16/128" and "They say: Surely God is with us" 9/41. In this case, if the Tatars (Mongols) had joined our group, there would have been love among us (Per. 136 / Tur.207).

(*Shariah*) (The Revealed Islamic Law) and the Sufi Path (*Tariqa*):

If you are looking for the reality of the revealed law then they are both true: the Shariah as well as Tariqa. The reality of the Shariah is like a lamp and the aim of the lamp is to show you the way in darkness, and you can trust your lamp. You can fix a wick in it and hang it up to illuminate the environment, but if you don't go on a path then what is the use of it? How can you get to a reality by staying at the same place? You ought to reach the Reality by walking on the path (Tur. 236).

Adversities are not without spiritual prosperities:

How can adversities enable people to be pious and righteous? If there is no pain, ego becomes a curtain. So it is essential that one who has no pain or worries must suffer some to avoid devastation. Prophet Muhammad said, "He who broadens his life (and knowledge), God broadens it further" (Per. 249 / Tur.55).

Why sometimes prayers are delayed?

It is said that angels plea to God, "Our Lord, there is a believer who is crying for help. You help even an infidel then why don't you help that poor fellow and answer his prayers?" God says, "Let me alone with my slave (lover). You can't be more merciful than Me. I love him and I like his yearnings. It is the part of love. There is a time when my lovers find it cumbersome to remember Me and they are hesitant to do so. Their words bounce backward and when they fail to admire God they feel disappointed. Crying sometime pleases them and sometime makes them upset, and so is the case with laughing. Once the preacher Shams-i Khajandi was crying for the family (of Muhammad who were murdered in Kerbela) and we were crying for him. Why was he crying for the family that had met with God and didn't cry over him (for not being with God). If he knew his own state, he would cry for himself and bring all the people of Damascus to cry and pray for him. There is no change in God, but it is always in you for instance, sometime you like bread and sometime you don't. There is a time when you like your friend and adore him, and sometime you hate him. If you could keep your previous (real) state and maintain yourself, you would become a mature person loved and sought by all. What is meant by maturity? Well it means that you see the reality clearly (Per. 271 / Tur.II.77).

All understand in accordance with their capacity of intellect:

"The beloved offers beauty and faithfulness in accordance with the degree of love". What does this mean? Every one seems to understand the above statement but within the capacity of their minds. When someone hears something he comprehends and evaluates it according to his experience and knowledge. So beware! When you hear some commentary or remarks on some subject it is the personal experience of that commentator (Per. 217 / Tur. II.25).

It is easier to know God than to know people:

To understand these people is more difficult than to understand God. You can know God by means of some hints. For example, you see a carved piece of wood and you can understand that there is someone who has carved it and shaped it because it cannot do it on its own. But when you look at people you see that they look like you outwardly, but they have a different world of their own, which is above your comprehension and understanding. It is easy to estimate the greatness of the carver of the wood by looking at his art. But only the experts (lovers of God) can tell you the greatness and delimitation of the artist (God) (Per. 219 / Tur.II.28).

Don't waste your time on philosophical discussions of how and why?

Don't bother yourself with "You say like this, and the others say like that or you think like this while others think like that". Why should you care for the eternity of the universe, you should try to learn about your own eternity. Find out whether you are eternal (*Kadim*) or mortal being (*Hadis*) by fate. You have a short age spend it on research. Why do you spend your life on useless discussion of eternity of the universe? Knowing God needs a deep study. But you are yourself deep, o negligent! If there is any depth, it is in you. What kind of a friend (of God) are you that you don't know the secret of your Beloved in your veins and fate as evident as the palm of your hand. How can you claim to be God-loving man if you don't know His secrets in you (Per. 283 / Tur.II. 87).

Whatever is created is good:

There is nothing ugly or bad in this world to some extent. Even infidelity is not bad unless compared with faith. In the presence of faith it looks abominable. For instance, iron is strong and useful metal, but when it is compared with brass it looses its value because brass is easily convertible and is more useful for chemical purposes than iron. Similarly, silver is a precious metal but has less value as compared to gold etc.(Per.170 /Tur. 343).

Note: From Islamic mystic point of view whatever God has created is positive, especially when you look at it through God's eyes.

All others than fish are soon fed up of water:

It is known that the fish live in water. If any of them run away from water or are afraid of it, they are not real fish. Similarly, if an atheist is told about God, he runs away and is scared of Him, and therefore wants to get out of water (divine love). But the fact that fish lives in water does not change even if it comes out of water for some time (Per. 170 / Tur. 344).

Note: Rumi gives the same idea in his 17th verse of Masnevi:

Everything except fish is sated with water,
He who has no daily bread, has hard time.

(Only those who have tasted God's love and His mercy are like fish in water, they can't do without it)

22. On Fasting:

Month of Ramazan (the fasting moth) is the only month for refinement. Public believe that God is more Kind and Protector during that month, but God has been Kind and Protector ever since God was there. So, why they say so and avoid sins? In reality, God is Kind during all the months (Tur. 293).

Eating less improves your esoteric powers:

Those whose target for bowing is kitchen,
Be informed, their future is in Hell.

(Per.168 /Tur.341).

Eating less makes wisdom grow,
Eating much makes wisdom slow.

If you don't eat much listen to this:

When you are here (in this world) and eat less, then keep your hunger for the other world and think that this the starting point. Learn this so that you may earn God's favor (*Savab*), spiritual broadness and see your Beloved's face. There are two kinds of people who fast: Those who have no food for eating and those who have plenty to eat but they don't eat for sake of God's favor (they are the true lovers of God) (Per. 168 / Tur. 341-352).

Generosity:

When Sultan Mahmud of Ghazna fell behind from his army, being very hungry, he said to a miller, "Hi, do you have something to eat? The miser miller thought, "Well this man has come to ask for bread (like others). From where has this parasite showed up?" Then he replied to the Sultan, "I have some left-over bread, will you eat it?" The Sultan said, "Alright fetch it". The miller went off and on the way he become reluctant and upon his return he said to the Sultan, "Unfortunately no bread has been left, if there was any bread, we would eat. Will you like to have some flour?" "Yes, bring whatever you have for eating" replied the great Sultan. Now, the miller realized that the man was really very hungry and would eat even the flour. So he came back and said, "Sorry, the flour is mixed up with millet and it belongs to a poor orphan". Finally he brought a salted piece of sheepskin and threw it in front of the Sultan and said, "This is all I have got"... The Sultan left that location in despair. On the way he came across a Turkish young boy, whom he asked, "Do you have something to eat?" "Yes, I do have, but first greet me (saying Salam Alaykum=May peace of God be on you) and then say, "May I be your guest!" The Sultan thought the boy was right, so he turned up and came back to say, "Hi, can I be your guest?" The boy offered bread (baked in ashes) yogurt, milk and cheese to his guest. The Sultan gave him a ring and said, "I am a close friend of the Sultan and you can for anything from him, and if he does not give you what you want, I will take from him and give you. When he saw the beautiful ring, he thought it would have been better to slaughter a sheep and had offered him (as a Turkish custom). He was sorry not to do so. However, the poor boy thought like that but his fate was soon to change. When the Sultan joined his army and marched on, the boy reached them and showed Sultan's ring to the soldiers. They all bowed to him for respect and soon he found the Viziers and generals all lined up to welcome him. He looked for the Emir and when he saw the Sultan in his real dress, he said to himself, "O my God, he was the Shah whom I had served the food!" The Sultan ordered forty slaves with golden belts to serve him. Well the rest you can guess how great the feast would have been.

Then the Sultan summoned the miller to his presence. One hundred armed soldiers went to bring him. They met the miller near a mountain. They asked, "Is he the miller?" People replied, "Yes, he is the man you are looking for". Seeing them the miller became terrified and ran to his house and locked the door. When the soldiers knocked at the door, he kept silent for some time and finally he said,

"I am already dead". The soldiers said, "What kind of dead are you that you can speak?" "This is my last breath, I am about to die" was the reply. Then the soldiers insisted, "Come out, let's go". Subsequently, they broke down the door and told him that the Sultan wanted him. The miller began to plea, "I am a poor miller what the great Sultan has to do with me? Well, if he has wheat, I can do my best for him". The soldiers said, "Don't speak nonsense, get up and let's get out of here". The miller said again, "Let me offer you nice bread and yogurt that even the Sultan couldn't have offered you". (You see now he is ready to entertain even a hundred guests). Finally, when he refused to go, they tied him up and dragged him to the Sultan. He looked around to find the chamberlain, but he saw the Sultan upon which the miller said, "I would not be able to save my head even if I had a hundred of them". When the Sultan heard this, he said, "Man, I have brought you here to take out my ring from the well." Then the Sultan ordered his men to tie him up and give him nothing to eat (in the well) for three days. The fellow was in habit of feeding his big belly with tons of bread every day. The man finally gave up hope for his life, and then the Sultan ordered his soldiers to bring him. "Now, what do you want, I have no breath left", said the miller to the soldiers, who said to him, "No, you will not die; you are a kind of person that you will not die at once". The soldiers took him to the Sultan, who asked the miller, "Man! Tell me will you eat rice one by one?" "Yes, I will eat even that way if I could find some", said the miller. The Sultan asked again, "What about eating a boiled well-fed bird seasoned with cumin or sugarcane? What about some dates?" "Oh, Why shouldn't I" said the miller. "We could also eat them if we could get some" added the Sultan. Then the Sultan began to name many dishes one by one, while the miller begged the Sultan to kill him. Upon this Sultan's heart softened and he remembered these lines from Khayyam's poetry:

I do wrong and You give me wrong in return,
Then what difference is there between You and me?

The Sultan began to laugh. He ordered to give the miller one hundred *Dirhems* and a dress and let him go. As the miller was to leave, the Sultan called him back. Now the miller thought that the Sultan was cheating him and he would punish him with something worse. The Sultan said, "Now, you have signed a contract with us that even if you do not give anything to others, at least you will not throw a sheepskin smothered with flavor on people's face as you did to me". He fell down in repentance and said, "Another thing that can be added to the contract is that I would never fail to entertain my guests or belittle them" (Per. 184 /Tur. 362).

Note: The above story is important from these points of view:

It reflects Mahmud of Ghazna's (who ruled India between A.D. 998 and 1030) character.

It shows that Turkish and Persian were spoken in that part and the Turk's hospitality was famous as usual.

The legendary verse of Khayyam quoted above was also known among people at the time of Shams.

24- Wasting time is also a sin:

Go and search for a beautiful beloved, and if you haven't become a perfect lover, look for another one. There are many beauties concealed under veils "There are yet many charming beauties to make you slave". Stop for rest, and have freedom from food and dress. Well, I don't have worries. God provides me all I need, and I have no love (desires) for that. The Koran says, "The spendthrifts are companions of Satan". Actually those who go to taverns and spend some coins are not the real spendthrifts, but those who spend their precious lives in negligence, which is the source of utmost felicity, and they know that the sun will decline one day (life will com to an end). There is no doubt about it, but they sleep away their time. Have they come to this world to spend their time for sleeping? (Per. 210 / Tur. 19).

25- Find a good fellow traveler:

There is a proverb, "First a good friend then a good path". What kind of a friend is required for a special path? This whole universe has created curtains and veils around human beings. God's chair, seven heavens, the world, the body of man and souls of animals are covers over covers. These curtains over curtains take us to the divine knowledge and the knower of God (Gnostic) is also a cover in relation to his Beloved, but he too has no value in the presence of his Beloved (Per. 265 / Tur. II.71).

26-Give alms to those who deserve it:

One coin (pence) you give to a God loving man is better than a hundred coins given to others, because that coin will be spent for a good cause. Hasn't God said in the Koran, "Give loan to God". It is said that God has hands in this sense, because when you give the alms to the needy ones it falls in God's hands especially when you help a God loving man. A Godly man is a slave of God and he is His part. There can be no totality without its part (Per. 264 /Tur.II.71).

27- We are all parts of the same whole:

Praise is to God! Everything is dedicated to man and man has dedicated his being to himself. God does not say in the Koran, "I have honored the skies and the Throne". Instead He says, "I have honored the sons of Adam.. (17/70) If you go to the Throne of God (*Arsh)* or far beyond there is no avail or you go seven layers under the earth there is no avail. It is your heart that opens to God. All the prophets and saints labored and suffered for it. The entire universe is in you, and if you know yourself you know all. Tatarism (Mongolism) is also in you. It is the attribute of violence. God says, "Lead my people to the right path because they don't know" which may also mean 'Show the path to my parts'. They (Mongols) were infidel, but they were also a part of the One. There can be no totality without its parts (as already said) (Per. 267-8 /Tur. II.73).

Note: Shams had no special favor for the Mongols, whom he calls 'infidel' but he says all human beings are parts of each other. They carry the same soul as is said in the Koran "I breathed into him (man) my spirit.."(15/28).

28- Death is not the final goal:

Men (of God) apologize once in their lives and for this, they repent only once. Someone was crying because the Mongols had killed his brother. He was a wise man. I said to him, "If you are wise then know that Mongols have given him eternity by killing him (made him martyr). These are the priests who are actually dead. What do they know about the life after death? They come to a stage and begin to shout. The Prophet (Muhammad) said, "This world is a prison for the believers" Now why should one cry for a prisoner who got freedom? Should people cry for this? The Mongols have made a hole in the prison and let him out. He has been transformed from this world to the other (Per. 268 /Tur.II.74).

29- It is the sincere submission that counts:

A Jew, Christian and a Muslim were friends. While traveling together they found a piece of gold and they cooked sweet (*Helva*) then they said, "It is not the right time, we can have it tomorrow, moreover this sweet is not enough for all of us. He who has a good dream can have it all". The purpose was not to give it to the Muslim friend. The Muslim got at midnight. It is difficult for a lover of God and a poor man to sleep soundly. He thought he could sleep any time, but the sweet may not be available again. So, he ate all of it. In the morning the Christian said, "Jesus came down and took me to Heaven." The Jew said, "Moses took me to Paradise and showed me around. That was wonderful!" The Muslim said, "The Prophet Muhammad came and said to me, "O poor fellow! The Christian has been taken to the fourth heaven and Moses took the Jew to Paradise. You are helpless and needy, so get up and eat the sweet". On this I woke up and ate the sweet. The others said, "By God your dream was the truest one and ours was only imagination" (Per.210 / Tur.II.20).

30- Metamorphosis of humankind:

It is a Hadis (the words of Muhammad) that there are twelve animals (monkey, pig, dog, elephant, wolf, mouse, lizard, scrab, turtle, fox, hedgehog, and bear) that were once human beings but they were metamorphosed into above animals because of their sins. Interpreters take the exoteric meaning of this Hadis and do not think about its esoteric meanings (Per. 213 / Tur. II.21).

Note: Many Hindus will agree with the above statement. It is interesting to notice that there is a verse in the Koran with the similar meaning: "Be ye apes despised and rejected" 2/65. Shams suggests that we should take them as symbols. However, some people carry the attributes of those animals in their lives.

31- One-hour's contemplation is better than sixty years' prayers:

The above words of Prophet Muhammad means the contemplation practiced in the company of a pious dervish who has no show. Doubtlessly, such a supplication is far better than the one performed openly without peace of mind. One can postpone the ritual prayers but one cannot postpone a dervish's company (Per.272 / Tur. II 78).

32- God-loving men must avoid blasphemy:

It is not decent to utter blasphemous words. When someone claims, "I am the Reality (God)" they abandon Muhammad's path and their words spread among public (all misunderstood). Therefore, even if dogs utter such words, they deserve execution unless they repent (Per. 274 /Tur. II.80).

33- How to have a meal?

Someone requested me, "Please, teach me etiquette of eating". I suggested him, "Eat in such a way that food should worry, but not you. It should not make you feel heavy, while you should make the food feel heavy (by giving it a hard time)". Then he invited me to have dinner with him. "I have no authority, God has the authority to tell you whether to eat or not, because He will suffer with you (Per. 335 /Tur. II.155).

34- Tears wash away your inner filth:

The smallest speck of spiritual filth is a thousand times worse than the physical filth. What kind of water cleans the inner filth? Only a few drop of tears. Not all sorts of drops, but the drops of your tears that come out of sincerity and righteousness (Per. 57 / Tur. 95).

35- On knowledge:

People go to school with the idea that they may learn languages and science with the aim that they may enter another college. To avail of time and opportunity, they choose a subject for discussion in meetings in order to gain fame. Why should one study to earn one's living? What is the use of the knowledge that does not tell you who you are and what is your value; and where shall you go after death and why are you here in this world and to where do you really belong? If this knowledge is like water in a jar, then you may look for the water regardless of jar. The purpose of learning Arabic or knowledge should be focused on: "By Kabba or tavern I mean nothing else but You" (Per.244 /tur. II. 50).

O you who have been lost in undoing the knot! Man has been created for the purpose that he may know where he has come from and where he is bound to. Exoteric and esoteric senses have been given to be used for this aim. However, people use these senses for other (minor) purposes. They don't seek protection to be happy and comfortable and to learn their past and present (the beginning and the end). Gaining knowledge, which is the best occupation, consumes time and the real aim is forgotten. The best preachers say this at the end of their lives: "The outcome of this world is nothing but sins and torture" which is a good advice for the entire world (Per. 247 / Tur.II.53).

36- God does not like the self-centered:

Whenever Bayazid set for Haj (pilgrimage), he preferred to go alone. He wouldn't like to accompany an unsuitable person. One day he saw a man, who had set out in front of him. When Bayazid looked at him, he liked his smooth walk. It occurred to him that he could join him and gave up the habit of traveling alone. He could be a nice company if he could be his friend for sake of God. When Bayazid was still thinking, the man turned his to him and said, "First find out whether I will allow you to travel with me or not?" and the mind reader went off lowering his head (Per. 290 / Tur.II.94).

37- First deserve then desire:

Whatever difficulties you face think it is because of you. God treats his slave (lover) in accordance with his value. Whatever the slave does, God does the same. Such being the case, there are all good things ready to be given (just deserve it) (Per. 294/Tur.II.98).

Note: If you want mercy of God, be merciful to others. if you don't want God to be angry with you don't be angry with others (see also the Essence of Rumi, p. 348) and Rumi adds:

If you need mercy, then take pity on the person shedding tears,
If you need mercy, then take pity on the weak and helpless.

(M I/380)

38- Training may be harsh, but the fruit is sweet:

A man was digging a piece of land when someone came and said, "Why are you digging this sound and healthy piece of land?" He didn't know what was bad and good for land. If the farmer didn't turn up the soil it would go bad and there would be no crops (torture for discipline may seem to be tough, but the result can be good) (Per. 295 /Tur. 98).

39- All the enlightened are friends of each other:

Some philosophers give preference to angels over prophets, and think that Prophet Muhammad and others are not as perfect as angels because they deal with common people. However, it is not true. Angels help the prophets to divert their attention to people in order to give them advice (preach them). This then does not mean that prophets forget God. They (the philosophers) also claim that they accept some miracles of prophets that are logical, and the illogical ones they deny. Intellect is the testimony of God, and God's testimony never contradicts. Well, I say that the miracle is above one's conception while intellect is the proof of God. Now, if you don't use intellect properly, it may seem to contradict. It is for this reason that people differ in many ways. For instance you can ask two persons, "How many two are there in two?" The answer will be "One" by both because it is an easy question. But if you ask, "How many seven are in seven or how many seventeen in seventeen?" they will be confused. This is because they reply recklessly without forcing their intellect. It is like holding a mirror in the wrong way. Once they hold it wrong all other mirrors go wrong in their views although they may be straight as is said in the Koran, "And unto thee We have revealed the scripture with the truth confirming whatever scripture was before it...5/48. "Lights are all friends of each other". Suppose that there is a group of one hundred people standing under the sunlight and watch a man who is coming towards them dancing and playing a drum. They will all agree. But if the same man comes at night, there will be a lot of discussion and contradiction among that group. Some will say, "There is an army approaching" while others will say, "No, it is a celebration party on the eve of circumcision", and so on. The philosophers may think that way about prophets, but the fact is that they are all part of the same light (Per.260 / Tur. 66).

40- Know your real friend and foe:

If you knew the difference between an enemy and a friend,
You would have lived the life twice,
There are many enemies with friendly faces,
Real friendship requires sharing of woes.

Well, the second life is for him, who hasn't died from the first and hasn't found the new body yet. He who succeeds to get the second life as the Koran says, "We shall make him live a better life and pay him recompense in proportion to the best of what he used to do" 16/97. He looks with the light of God and, therefore, is able to see the difference between a friend and foe. He oppresses when oppression is required and he is kind when kindness is required. Both these attributes lead him to the target. We need the characters of Muhammad and his cousin Ali to reform this nation, who had severity and kindness at the same time (Per. 372 /Tur. II.171).

41- Unity of hearts:

It is ordered to the Muslims that they should prostrate in prayers towards Ka'ba. Now, suppose all the nations of the entire world are there (around Ka'ba) and we lift up the Ka'ba from the center, they all would be prostrating each other. That is they are worshipping each other's hearts (Per. 212 /Tur.II. 20).

A person had filed suit and witnesses were required. He took ten witnesses to the Cadi, who said, "Bring one more (who is not from your sect)". The man reminded him this verse from the Koran: "And call to witness, from among your men, two witnesses" 2/382. "Sir, I have brought ten already". The Cadi said, "They are all one and you bring a thousand more, they will be the same (Per. 327 /Tur.II.130).

42- Separation dims the light of love:

I looked at the preserved tablet (*Lavh-i Mahfuz* = the tablet of divine program) and I saw a crowd of people and a man in the middle who had given up his religion, and the Persian poems were being written and exchanged, which was really a good fun in the company of friends. They showed their lovely faces to each other, but those who fall apart from such a company loose their light (liveliness) because air comes between them, like a thing that you preserve in honey and when you take it out (separate) it goes bad (Per. 326 / Tur. II. 129).

43- This world is like a snake:

Someone was complaining about the people of this world. Others said to him, "This world is a game and comedy for the mature, while it is no game and is a serious thing for children. Now, if you want to avoid this game and comedy just don't play. Well, if you want to play with it, then eat, drink and enjoy yourself for crying is not the part of the game but laughing is. This world is the treasure and snake. Some play with the treasure and some with the snake. Those who play with the snake must tolerate its bites as it bites you with its head or its tale. If the snake attacks you with its tale, and you don't wake up it can bite you by its head (mouth). The people who have got rid of this burden (of materialistic desires) and follow an old experienced man (a Sheikh or a Priest) because the wisdom of that man is like an emerald in the eyes of the snake. When a dragon-like snake sees the old man leading his followers, it looses its power. Then the snake that was like crocodile in water turns into a bridge under your feet. Its poison changes into sugar and its thorns into roses. The way layer becomes a guide, and the fear a source of peace and protection. Universal wisdom is like an experienced bowman who can draw the string to its full while the worldly intellect has a servile nature and fails to draw the string of the bow fully and therefore, it is weak and helpless. The mundane intellect utters words from its mouth and the universal intellect utter words from the depth of its heart. It is referred in the Koran: "Had it been possible for a lecture to cause the mountains to move, or the earth to torn asunder or the dead to speak (this Koran would have done so) Nay, but God is the whole command 13/31

The words that have no meaning in one's mind
Writing and speaking of those words are in vain.

(Per.364 / Tur.II.164).

Man should look back and forward to check out if there is a wall or a barrier of the love of the world as is said, "Loving the worldly things make you deaf and blind". When love of things overcomes religious feelings, blindness and deafness occur and the Koran says this, "We made among their hands and behind them barriers." However, if one repents over his sins and wakes up, (God will certainly forgive). When love of this world abates, the barriers also disappear, and this is generally obtained by talking to pious people who have no bad feelings (Per. 365 / Tur. II.164).

44- How to cope up with scandals?

If someone says that there is a person who is praising you, tell him that actually you want to praise me by an excuse. If someone tells you that a person is calling your names, tell him that these are your words, and this is the result of your own feelings. May be the person who swore you didn't really say what the narrator has said. If a person tells you that a man is jealous of you, tell him that there is a double meaning of jealousy: One kind of jealousy takes you to Paradise and is cherished by the person who wants to be like you and doesn't want to fall behind in good deeds. The other is against the lovers of God, which does no harm to them in the sense that the lovers of God are always worried for others' problems, and those who are jealous and try to hinder the men of God, they only lessen their heavy burdens. (Per. 366 / Tur. II.165).

45- Heart is the location of divine light:

One should not depend on his temperament but on heart. So, one should look for a heart and not for the nature. Heart has a trap because heart is hidden behind a veil. People call a lover 'owner of the heart' for the sake of jealousy; otherwise he is the owner of God. When the shadow of divine light falls on heart, the heart becomes extremely delighted. When all of a sudden that light fades away, and it happens many times like that, the heart begins to melt away and disappears to leave the space for God (Per.338 /Tur. 140).

The Prophet David once asked God, "Where can I find you?" God replied, "I may not be accommodated in the earth or in the heaven, yet I can be accommodated in the hearts of the believers", and God added, "I am with those who are heart broken for Me". We call those heart- broken ones "the possessors of heart" and God loves such hearts but sincerity comes first. When they reach God, they shine with His light yet hey are kept secret (Per. 338 / Tur. 140).

Note: In the Islamic mysticism 'heart' has a long definition. However, a short one will be "a treasure of divine secrets having four main curtains: 1-*Sadr* (the chest) that receives God's inspirations 2- *Qalb* (the heart) the location of divine light 3- *Fawad* (the soul) curtain of divine disclosures 4- *Shghaf* (core of heart) the store of divine love (for other details see Farhang-i Jafar, p.212).

On the Holy Koran:

These are Muhammad's words, "There are some when they read the holy Koran, it curses them". Here Muhammad used the word '*rubba*' which means 'some' therefore it does not include all the readers. Those who are not included are the special lovers of God and are believers of the Koran. They know seven (multi) meanings of the Koran. As is said by Muhammad, "The Koran has esoteric as well as exoteric meanings and for the esoteric there are seven layers." As these seven interpretations change according to the culture and customs of people, they belong to common people but the lovers of God (Saints) know many other (tens and thousands) meanings of the Koran. Such lovers of God are not mentioned in the

Koran openly but by allusion, and they are above all other groups (Per. 111 /Tur.171).

Note: For example see Mulla Sadra's and Ikhwan ul-Safa's commentaries.

God says in the Koran. "We shall show them our portents on the horizons (further regions of the universe) and in their own soul, until Truth becomes manifest to them..." 41/53 What is meant by this verse? Does it mean the splitting of the moon (Muhammad's miracle) or the summer season? God says further "In their own soul". Does this mean health and sickness? These can all be positive interpretations of the verses dear interpreters. Beside the above interpretations 'in their own soul' can also mean the broadening of their chests with divine knowledge. Doubtlessly, 'Analhaq' means 'God is the Truth' or even 'Muhammad is the truth'. This interpretation is also nice, but it belongs to the walkers of the divine path. Every verse of the Koran is like a love letter and gives good news. Lovers of God know the Holy Koran. The beauty of the Koran attracts them and plays with them. As far as 'Analhaq'= I am the reality' is concerned, which also means 'I am the real interpretation of the Reality' we don't need Tusi's interpretations as long as the 'Qudsi' (divine knowledge) is with us. As God says, "The Beneficent God. It is He Who has taught the Koran" 55/1. So you can hear the Koran's commentary from God. In case you hear others commentaries, they are theirs and as simple as a five years old child can understand it (Per. 187 /Tur.366).

Note: Tusi (Perhaps Firdavsi Tusi is meant, who was a great Persian poet of the 10th century and famous for his 'Shah Nama'). The portents or signs of God in the horizons (universe) have already leaded us further into the universe by scientific researches. This gives wider meaning to the verse.

(Someone asked) what is meant by this Koranic verse: "Companions restrained (as to their glances), in pavilions whom no man or even Jinn before them has touched" 55/71 and 74. "Don't be silly, this kind of beauty exists only in the world of God", said I. He said, "Even one can think about that". I added, "There are beauties in the world of God, whom neither human kind nor Jinn have reached (seen) nor drinks of that world like pure wine, camphor, ginger or water springs are found here (their similitude is incomparable) (Per. 232 /Tur. II.39-40).

Ibn Mesud narrates that the Prophet Muhammad used to explain the meanings of the Koran. He explained one meaning to his friends (*Ashab*) and the other one to me, and if I had disclosed that meaning to them, they would have certainly killed me, because it was a custom to kill a person who spoke blasphemy (ibid).

There was a man who desired to learn the Koran. He had difficulty in memorizing it and looked for a teacher who could teach him properly, and for this he even prayed to God to find one. Suddenly, he heard that there was a teacher in Baghdad, who could meet his requirement. He went to the teacher and recited the verses he knew by heart. The teacher corrected him. He realized that he was an excellent teacher and he had wasted his time before in search of a teacher. The teacher said, "Well if you want to learn the Koran properly, you have to pay me one Dinar of gold for each section as my father has told me". The learner agreed to that. The sessions continued while the learner kept on paying regularly. Finally, he had no Dinars left and was really sorry. He saw an old man who asked him, "Why are you so sad, my son?" When the learner explained his situation to him, the old man began to laugh and invited him to his house, and offered him good food but the learner couldn't eat in comfort because he was very sorry. Consequently, the old man told him that he was the teacher's father, and that he had deposited all the golden coins in a bag. Then he said, "My son does not need your coins the prophet Muhammad says: 'He who does not read the Koran properly is not one of us', so our gold is the Koran and our property is also the Koran. We have learnt from the Koran that we should not depend on others but on the Koran. We did so to test you. Here are all of your coins we got from you. Take them and you are free to leave. If you had not indulged into those ideas, we wouldn't have tested you and we need not ask for the donkey foal (valueless gold coins) (Per. 311 / Tur.II. 114).

God says in the Koran, "..and whoever hopes for meeting with his Lord, let him do righteous work, and make none sharer of the worship due unto his Lord 18 / 110. This means that He is the only One God, and there is none equal to His Being and "God leads to reality with His light to those whom He wishes" 24/35. These promises and punishments mention in the Koran belong to other people because some are forgiven (the selected ones). Someone said, "Why do you offer five time prayers?" The other replied, "Because God has ordered to do so". "Well, He hasn't said so He says, O ye who believe! Do not draw near to prayer when you are drunk" 4/42. The man said, "You may take it that way. All the verses are according to some particular circumstance. Some time it tells you the situation of believers and some time of the infidel. But in the world of love there is always kindness and no torture". We (Sufis) have come out of the range of anger of God, which is close by and Hell is beside. When you pass by Hell you are on the way to Paradise. The world of God's Mercy is limitless (Per.228 /Tur.II.35).

They told me to write a commentary on the Koran. I said to them, "You know how my commentary is. It doesn't seem to suit either the Prophet Muhammad or God. It even refuses me (suit me). I say to the commentary, "As you deny me, set me free, go, and why do you give me headache?" But it keeps on staying with me and refuses to leave me. Even my ego does not understand my words (commentaries). It is like a scribe who writes three different kinds of writings: one, only he can read it and no one else, second he and others can read. The third one is the kind, which neither he nor others can read. So whatever I say, neither others nor I understand (because it does not belong to me but God). Some verses, however, seem to need no explanation and can be ignored, but as a matter of fact they are the ones that need explanation (Per. 326 / Tur. 129).

PARABLES

1- The man who fell in love with a brick:

There was a man who looked for a God-loving man. He listened to many Sheikhs' sermons but no spiritual door was opened on him. One day he found a brick and laid his head on that, and went to sleep. When he was asleep, divine secrets were disclosed to him. As soon as he woke up, he took the brick, kissed it and put it under his arm. After that wherever he went he took the brick with him. He wouldn't offer prayers without the brick. If he went to visit a friend or to condole with him or to join a party or go to sleep, he would never be without the brick. If someone praised him, he would tell him to praise the brick first, which had the value of diamond for him, and if somebody shook hands with him, he would tell him to hold the brick first. If anyone asked, "What is it under your arm?" He would say, "What is it not? Whatever is good comes from it and whatever is bad goes. It has been thirty years that I have been in search for something, and when I put my head on it, I found what I was looking for".

Lover, o sweet heart! This idea never came to my mind,
That I should give up hope of meeting with you,
I was free from worries, but the fate didn't like it,
I was so happy with you, but the time didn't like it.

(Per. 310 / Tur.II.112).

2- The Mouse and the Camel:

A mouse caught the bridle of a camel and began to draw it. The camel followed the house patiently out of courtesy, mildness and sympathy. As Muhammad said, "The believers are like the bridled camels (submissive)". Some say that 'camel' in this Hadis stands for obedience and modesty, while some say it is a symbol of height and loftiness. If this is all wrong, then there is another meaning hidden and understood according to one's own capacity of comprehension. When they came to a riverbank, the mouse who thought that he was fast and great stopped desperately. The camel said, "Why have you stopped here, can't you go any further? Why didn't you realize it before that this is not a kind of job for you? Now that you have my bridle in your hand you must proceed". The mouse said, "The water is too deep to go on". The camel went into water up to his knees and said, "It is shallow here". The mouse replied, "Sir, it depends on the length and height of the legs". "Now, be repentant and don't be impudent the next time. Come and settle down on crupper of my saddle where tens and thousands of mice like you can be accommodated and I can safely take them all to the other side of the river" (Per. 228 / Tur. II.36).

Note: The main idea is that God loving men are bestowed by divine enlightenment by birth. They are patient and kind like the camel, and intelligence (the mouse) doesn't always control them.

3- A mule and a camel:

A mule said to a camel, "How can it be fair that you rarely come in front of the caravan while I am generally in front?" The camel replied, "Well dear! I am courageous and I have a long neck and a high head with two shining eyes. I can look far enough and see which place is steep and which is shallow" (Per. 241 /Tur.II.47).

4- Epistle of the birds:

All birds set out to see *Simurgh.* They flew over the seven seas. Some lost their lives because of the severe cold, others fell down into water or the marine smell killed them. In the end, only two of the birds were left. They were filled with pride to find that they were safe and began to look for Simurgh. As soon as they saw him, blood came out of their beaks and they died (physically). However, the Simurgh is still perched over the mountain *Qaf,* and only God knows to where shall it fly? All birds aspire to reach that great bird but many die. They claim to acquire the state of that bird. If they could ever receive the scent of that state once, their lives would completely change (Per. 276).

Note: The above tract is a reference to the 'Risalat al-Tayr' of Ibn Sina or Imam-i Ghazali's "Epistle of the Birds" where birds decide to find Simurgh to make him their king. Many perish on the way and only a few escape that have a chance to listen to their Lord (Simurgh). Simurgh said to the remnants, "I am already your sovereign and Lord, whether you like it or not, and I don't need your offer. Finally when the birds realized their mistake of not knowing their true Lord, they were forgiven and were given shelter. They later discovered to their surprise that none of the birds had perished on the way as is said, "Each one has a goal towards which he returns, so vie with one another in good deeds"(Risalat al-Tayr, Imam-i Ghazali, Book II p.148). A similar story is written by Feriduddin Attar.

5- Bayazid and a dog:

Bayazid of Bistam often went to Haj on foot (as already said). He had performed seventy Hajes. One day when he was on his way to Haj he noticed that people were very thirsty and were going to die. He saw a dog by the well, where the pilgrims had swarmed and they were oppressed. The dog looked at Bayazid. Just then he was inspired by God to find water for the dog. So he began to shout, "Who wants to buy Haj for one glass of water?" No one was interested in the offer. He shouted again, "OK for seven Hajes performed on foot or more even seventy" Someone agreed. A bit of pride fell in the heart of Bayazid, who thought that he had done a great job by selling seventy Hajes for the poor dog. When he poured the water in a pot and gave it to the dog, the dog just glared at him and refused to drink. Bayazid fell down on earth to beg to God. Finally he heard a voice: "You have been saying so far: 'I did this, I did that for God' and now you see even the dog hasn't accepted your water" He pleaded to God and said, "My Lord, I will not do that again, forgive me". Upon this the dog began to drink the water:

You are such a being that despite a hundred intercessions and cries,

You don't let me kiss at least one of your feet.

(Per. 278 / Tur.83-84).

6- The story of three princes:

A king had three sons, who were to set out for an important task. Their father gave them this advice many times: 'When you reach a castle just pass by it quickly and do not enter it. If the father didn't warn them, they would feel no desire to enter the castle. They began to wonder as what laid in the building, because it is said that man has more desire for forbidden things. They went in (as the story is well known) and saw the picture of king's daughter with which they all fell in love. They went to the king one by one and told him to marry the princess. The king ordered his men to show them the ditch where the heads of the dead laid (they were executed because they couldn't produce any token of love). The eldest son claimed to bring the token but he failed and was executed. The second one had the same destiny. When the smallest decided to try, the king told him to take a lesson from the fate of his brothers. But the boy said:

Patience has no way to love,
Patience does not help yearning,
It is a good thing to be patient,
Yet a loving heart listens to no admonition.

Now it happened that the princess' nanny took pity on the young boy for his loyalty. She advised the boy to make a golden cow and hide him in that, and with this trick he could enter the princess' room. People go to sleep but lovers stay awake because the love-light kills the night. When the night fell, the boy came out of the statue. The candles were lit and wine was served that wetted the locks of the girl. At daytime some signs were seen, but none knew the fact. The boy took one of her bracelets as a token and. The public was already convinced of his loyalty and elegance; they took the prince's side. The boy said to the people, "Don't worry, I have the token and when I show it to the king, he will die; and you can pull his legs and throw him out". The king asked, "Where is your token, show me". The boy said that he would do that only in the presence of the Vizier, and he would show him such a token that he would faint away ending all his doubts. When they came together in privacy, the boy produced the bracelet, a ring and other tokens:

Pains and worries all change into happiness by your kindness,

Life finds immortality when you cast your loving- eyes,

When the dust of your street is carried away by the wind towards Hell,

All the fire turns into sweet water of life.

(Per. 304 / Tur.II.108).

Note: This is the complete story, which has been left unfinished by Rumi because of his death in the last volume of his Masnevi. The lesson to be taken from the story is that perseverance takes one to success.

A man was sowing something at a place far from his house. People asked him, "Why don't you sow in your own land near your house?" The man said, "That land is barren and salty". My (Shams') words are useful and beneficial but there are many useful things that people do not make use of (Per. 69/ Tur.111).

There is a famous story of ten Sufis. One of them fell in love with a Christian girl and would follow her wherever she went, even to the Church. The girl asked, "Why are you after me?" The Sufi explained his situation. The girl said, "Look, we do not like to mix up with other nations and religions, then why should you expect anything from me?" Desperately, the Sufi explained his situation to his comrades about his love, and that he had decided once for all to go and buy a rope girdle to be a Christian. The friends said, "Let's go together and buy ten rope belts for all of us so that we act like one soul in ten bodies. When the girl saw them together, the Sufis told her about the situation and said, "Sufis are like one soul". The girl broke away her rope belt and said, "I have never seen such a unity in any nation or group of faith". Her parents and others reproached her and said, "How can you be cheated by these Sufis and change your religion?" The girl replied, "If you see what I see in him, you will fall in love with them ten times more" (Per. 71/ Tur.113).

Abu Bekir Rubabi (the Rubab player) had heard the fame of Juha (the Nasreddin Hoja of the Arabs). One day, they came across each other but did not recognize. Both had stolen a donkey, clothes and a pouch of a man. Being depressed, the man who was robbed hung a notice board on his chest saying, "I have been robbed" and he cried. Juha and Bekir stole that board as well. They soon became good bosom friends. They exchanged their arts and tricks. One would show trick of picking a pocket and the other would surpass him in many ways. One day, Bekir asked Juha, "Tell me the truth who are you in reality, and from where have you come to know these tricks?" The answer was, "I am Juha." Bekir said, "I believe that". Finally, they became a nice company of dervishes (humble friends) because they understood each other well.

Note: It is interesting to notice that Nasreddin Hoja of Turkey is a wise God-loving character or even a saint, who teaches moral by means of anecdotes. Juha of the Arabic world is a funny character, who would do anything for fun even steal and cheat while the Indian and Iranian character 'Molla Nasreddin' is nothing more than a wise funny man. The lesson that may be taken from the story is that one has to have a common taste to be good friends. Similarly, man has to have some attributes of God to be His friend as suggested by Ibn al-Arabi and Rumi (Per.72/ Tur.115).

A Muslim preacher (Hoja) was delivering a sermon on marriage. He quoted Hadises after Hadises to convince people in the congregation to get married. He requested women to get married and to married couples he requested to be matchmakers. Just then a man shouted, "A Sufi is the son of the moment" to try his luck he said, "I am a poor fellow yet I need a woman to marry". The preacher turned his face toward the women and said, "Is there anyone desirous among you to marry this gentleman?" "Yes here I am" said a woman. Then the preacher said, "Come closer to the pulpit and open your veil so that the man may see your face as the Canon orders". When she unveiled her face, the preacher told the man to tell his opinion. The man was positive upon which the preacher asked the woman, "What do you have as your income?" She replied that she had a donkey that carried water, took wheat to the mill or carry wood to provide her living. The preacher said, "No, this man looks like a noble one he cannot be your donkey driver, is there anyone else?" Another woman showed up and unveiled her face when the preacher asked, "Alright what do you have?" The woman gave this answer, "I have a bull. It turns the water wheel, ploughs the land etc." The preacher said, "This man is not fit for being a shepherd for your bull. Is there anyone else?" There rose a third woman, came to the culprit and unveiled the face. The preacher asked her the same question. She said that she had a garden. The preacher said, "Well, now it is up to you man to select any of these ladies". The man thought for a while and replied, "I would rather ride the donkey, lead the bull in my front and go to the garden". The preacher said, "Well man, you are not as precious as to marry all of them" (Per 73/ Tur.117).

Note: According to a belief (for instance of Juneyd of Bghdad) a Sufi should be 'A son of the moment=Ibn ul-Waqt' because to think about the past obsessively leads one to a false pride, while to think about the future continuously creates fantasy, and in both the cases one is cast away from God. Therefore, a Sufi must think about the present time that leads to Eternity that has no beginning and end. The above story is, however, an irony to the misunderstanding of the concept which may easily lead to opportunism.

A man brought an Indian sword as a present for his friend and said, "This is the famous Indian sword". The friend asked, "What is the Indian sword good for?" The man replied, "It cuts everything into two pieces". The friend said, "Well, I am 'Son of the moment', let's try it". He took the sword and tried it on a stone. The sword broke into two pieces instead of the stone. The friend said, "You told me that it can cut anything into two, now it has broken". The friend reply, "This is really an Indian sword but the stone is worse than the sword". Moses was more Pharaoh than the Pharaoh. Pharaoh was a God-loving man but Moses was more than that (Per.87 / Tur.136).

BIBLIOGRAPHY

Abdulbaki Gölpınarlı, *Mevlana Celaleddin*, Inkilap Kitabevi, Istanbul 1985.

Annemarie Schimmel, *The Triumphal Sun*, Fine Books London.

Turkish Ansacleokpedia of Islam and Urdu Daire-yi Maarif-e Islam, Punjab University.

Coleman Barks, *The Esssential Rumi*, Cattle Books 1997.

E.H.Whinfield, *Teachings of Rumi*, the Octagon Press, London.

Eflaki: Ahmed Dede, *"Manakib al- Arafin"* Tahsin Yazici, TTK, Ankara, 1959.

Erkan Turkmen, The Essence of Rumi's Masnevi, Ministry of Culture of the Turkish Republic of Turkey, 2002, Ankara.

…………………. *Şems-i Tebrezi'nin Öğretileri*, Nüve Kültür Merkezi, Konya 2009.

Ferhang, Dr. Seyyid Jafer, *Lugati Istilahat- u Tabirati Irfani*, Kutuphana-yi Tuhuri, Tehran.

Hilmi Ziya Ülken, *İslam Düşüncesi Tarihi*, Rızakoşkun Matbası Istanbul 1946.

History of Islamic Philosophy, Edited by Seyyed Hosein and Oliver Leaman, Routledge, London.

Khanbaba Mushar, *Abdurrahman bn Ahmed Jami*, Mulefin-i Kutube Chapi, Iran, v.i p. 430(Ghazali).

Per: *Maqalat-i Shams-i Tabrezi*, Ahmed Khushnawis, Tehran 1349.

Nafahat-ul Uns, Abdurrahman bn Ahmed Jami, Kiatb Farushi-yi Mahmudi, Iran.

W.Chittick, *The Sufi Path of Love,* State University of New York Press Albnay.

Tur: *Şems-i Tebrezi Konuşmaları* çeviren Nuri Gencosman, Hürriyet Yayınları Istanbul.

Franklin D. Lewis, *Past and Present, East and West, The Life, Teachings and Poetry of Jelal al_Din Rumi,* Oneworld Oxford, 2003.

Mak.M: Makalat-i Shams-i Tabrezi, Muhammed Ali Muvahhid, Chapkhane-i Diba,Tehran, Iran.

Mak.A: Makalat-i Shams-i Tabrezi, Ahmed Khushnavis, Tehran 1349.

W.Chittick, *Me & Rumi,* Fons Vitae, Canada 2004.

INDEX